964[a]

ALVIN C. GLUEK, JR.
350 WHITEHILLS DRIVE
EAST LANSING, MICH.

THE
QUEBEC REVOLUTION

FRENCH CANADIAN RENAISSANCE
SERIES

PIERRE LAPORTE
THE TRUE FACE OF DUPLESSIS

PIERRE JÉRÔME
THE IMPERTINENCES OF BROTHER ANONYMOUS

PAUL SAURIOL
THE NATIONALIZATION OF ELECTRIC POWER

HUGH BINGHAM MYERS
THE QUEBEC REVOLUTION

THE QUEBEC REVOLUTION

Hugh Bingham Myers

HARVEST HOUSE,
MONTREAL

A NOTE ON SOURCES

In the preparation of this volume, the author relied on French source materials. Unless otherwise indicated, the footnote page references at the back of the book are keyed to the original French publications. For the sake of consistency and for the benefit and information of the English reader, standard translations of French works have been used when available. In all other cases the translations are the author's.

First Printing April 1964

Copyright © Canada 1963 by Harvest House Ltd.
Library of Congress Catalog Card Number: 63-23107

Printed by HARPELL'S PRESS CO-OPERATIVE
Ste. Anne de Bellevue

CONTENTS

CONTENTS (Cont'd.)

Big Game

The Moderate

In the Great Tradition

The Balance Sheet

EDITOR'S INTRODUCTION

To many who welcomed the French-Canadian anti-parochial renaissance, the Quebec "revolution" comes like a kick in the groin.

With the "renaissance" we seemed on surer footing. We thought we were getting at the cultural and economic heart of the matter. The "French fact" as an intrinsically valuable force in Canadian life, and as a contribution to our uniqueness, has always had the support of thoughtful Canadians — even if it took a few riots and burnings in effigy to make it manifest to all. Want, lack of opportunity for education and satisfying employment are evils that we could understand — from our own experience — and cope with. The demagoguery that they have bred is another matter. The "Buy Quebec" form of tribalism, the disciplined and semi-disciplined cohorts, schooled in a foreshortened view of history, and on a smattering of social science are likely to be more trying.

In the midst of the present ambivalence in the Quebec "revolution" and the headless violence of the recent past, it is the great merit of Hugh Myers' book that he rarely lets us forget that the struggle between the two French Canadas is the paramount issue. The creative, rational, liberty-loving Quebec is ranged against the parochial, obscurantist, spoils-tolerant society of the past. Here is life and growth. The racist, and extreme nationalist overtones which threaten to smother the "Rite of Spring" from Quebec are the death throes of the old order which nurtured us.

Hugh Myers is a "typical English Canadian", as English as Cheshire cheese. Well, not quite. His father came from London and his mother from Derby. He is a Roman Catholic. The name Myers? It could be Central European. He grew up on an Alberta farm and graduated from a western university. In 1958, before the "revolution", he came freely to the famous Laval University summer school to study the French language.

In Quebec, he met and married a charming "French Canadian" girl. Hugh remained in Quebec City to teach English in the oldest boys' school in Canada and to contribute two hostages — a son and a daughter — to the future of Canada. With these children, two more "typical" Canadians are amongst us. If you ask me to which of the two "races" they will belong, I would bet on it — knowing the parents — that they will join the thin-skinned race, rather than the thick-skinned one.*

It was a fair wind, in an hour of need, that brought us an author who contradicts in his person the stereotypes of bigots in all the communities of this land. It is insight of a high order that has led him to select so aptly the events that illustrate the power and acceleration which the "revolution" is gathering.

Take the impact of the "revolution" when it was still a gangling colt, some five years ago, on that other fact, the *Canadian Fact*.

On the 24th of February 1959, Mr. L. J. Pigeon, Conservative M.P. from Joliette-l'Assomption-Montcalm, rose in Parliament at Ottawa on "the order of the day" and innocently asked:

"Will the question pertaining to the racial origin of Canadians be included in the census forms for the 1961 decennial census?"

The Honourable Gordon Churchill (Minister of Trade and Commerce), replied on behalf of the government:

"There will be a question asked in that census return just as in 1951 expressed in the words, 'What is your origin' which means what is your ethnic descent. To that question people may reply and these replies will be acceptable, *Canadian†*, English, French, etc."

The reply signified that those who were born in Canada, and, certainly those whose fathers were born in Canada, could simply say they were Canadians.

In the Province of Quebec, however, one has to take into account the very real fear of the French-speaking residents, surrounded by 200 million English-speaking North Americans, that their French language and French culture cannot survive except by determined, positive, and extraordinary provisions. The reply by Mr. Churchill, therefore, far from satisfying the spokesmen of Quebec, was the signal for a storm of protest against the admissibility of "Canadian" as a possible reply to the question: "What is your origin?"

---

* The words of the archeologist, Pierre Teilhard de Chardin, speak to their predicament (and ours) when he says: "I would like to make plain my faith in human work and human unity, my anger against the compartments and ceilings, which isolate fragments of spirits, destined to be joined together, our deception in seeing ourselves imprisoned in a cell whose limits exhaust us, our anguish in seeing ourselves alone, every one of us, in astronomical space." And, "I am dreaming of a sort of Book of the Earth in which I would speak not as a Frenchman or in any sectional interest but as Man or indeed Earth-born." See C. E. Raven, *Teilhard de Chardin: Scientist and Seer*, Collins, London, 1962, pp. 169 and 170.

† Italics ours.

The battle of ethnic origins on the census is but the contemporary version of the "battle of the cradles" of yesteryear. In order to win this particular battle, a so-called* French-Canadian (or *Canadien*), has to insist that no one else may describe himself as a Canadian. Otherwise, the power of his numbers, taken as a bloc, might not weigh so heavily in political manoeuvres, infighting at federal-provincial conferences, etc.

This view of things has become so ingrained that the most liberal, outward-looking Quebec citizen finds difficulty in detaching himself from it. It explains why an essentially separatist device was so wholeheartedly supported within the Provincial Government, the press, and in other influential quarters.

How was this question of ethnic origin looked upon elsewhere in Canada at this time and indeed by the leader of the Conservative party, Mr. Diefenbaker?

On July 4, 1960, Mr. J. R. Taylor, M.P. for Vancouver-Burrard, rose in the House of Commons to have his say on the census question. In the course of his address, he referred to Mr. Diefenbaker's own fight against "hyphenated citizenship and registration of Canadians according to paternal racial origin". He cited Mr. Diefenbaker's first address in the Commons, on this question. Said Mr. Diefenbaker:

"My criticism of the census is that, regardless of the number of generations that have elapsed or the admixtures of nationality that have taken place during 40, 50, 75, or 125 years, so long as persons must register under the nationality of their paternal ancestor, there will never be that Canadianism which we wish to establish." *And so it transpired.*

In spite of the enlightened view of the Prime Minister, the Conservative government bowed to the heat from Quebec, and in the 1961 census of Canada "each person was asked the question, 'To what ethnic or cultural group did you or your ancestor (on the male side) belong on coming to this continent?' The language spoken at the time by the person, or his paternal ancestors, was used as an aid in the determination of the person's ethnic group."†

Alas, we were not to be permitted to answer "Canadian" to the question on ethnic origin. Only such answers as "British Isles",

---

* I say, "so-called", only because French-speaking Canadians are as mixed in their origins as any of us and have, in fact, intermarried with most of us. They are North Americans with a difference, and *vive la différence!*

† *1961 Census of Canada,* Population, Ethnic Groups, by Age Groups. Bulletin 1. 3-2.

"French", "German", "Italian", "Jewish", "Netherlands", "Polish", etc., were permitted. Henceforward, it was our fate to be yoked like dumb, obedient cattle, each in its own stanchion, each with its own name plate — none bearing the name, Canada.

There is no time to lose in meeting by all practical means, the deeply-felt insecurity of French-speaking Canadians about the fate of their language and culture in North America. But the lesson of this *dénouement* is that it is fatal to the existence of our democracy as it contradicts its very essence — to pander to the supposed interests of any one group of Canadians at the expense of all.

The misguided policy of conceding principle for momentary political convenience — especially with respect to the principle of Canadian citizenship — is more responsible than any other single factor for extremism in Quebec to-day.

English-speaking extremists (it would not be inaccurate to call them separatists) who profess to see no reason why Canada should exist independently of the U.S.A. — who see nothing positive in Canada worth preserving, feed the fear of the French-speaking Canadians for the safety of their culture. This is the gap into which the French extremist-separatists have vaulted, and which they have filled, for, in essence, they have no loyalty to Canada, either. Their vociferous success, in turn feeds the impulse for making crass common cause with the U.S.A. A spirit of separatism rises higher in both English- and French-speaking groups. The will, on both sides, to establish and maintain a viable Canada has become a pre-condition for solving the present crisis between communities.

Fortunately, the "revolution" has its happier elements. The struggle for *independence and sovereignty* may serve as a necessary counterweight to the residue of colonial fact and the much larger residue of colonial mentality which persists in Canada — in our employment and investment policies, in our reading, and other habits.

Decentralization, another element in the "revolution" which Hugh Myers has emphasized, is potentially more democratic and humane. Potentially: because it may jeopardize general standards of welfare and block interregional economic planning and conservation; because the lesser unit of government everywhere tends to present a weaker target to giant corporations bent on having their way with resources and laws; because precious human relations and group associations of long standing may be severed.

Bill 60 may be seen as a long step toward the older, more genuine, more liberal Canadian (North American and Continental) tradition of the common school.* It is the separate school, above all, which has artificially divided Canadians in Quebec, as well as in the West. It has left us powerless to utilize our French (Catholic) teachers to teach the much-needed French in our English (Protestant) schools, and vice-versa. It has left other citizens totally without a voice in the formal education of their children.

In the pages of Hugh Myers' book which sharply reflect the "revolution", we encounter an editor's plea for justice — not just French-Canadian justice — but eternal justice for the non-French-speaking Anglican, Wilbert Coffin. This too is of the essence of democracy.

Among the many gracious actors in the "revolutionary" drama are the labour leaders who are anti-racist and non-nationalist, the professors who plead eloquently for common humanity, the editors who eschew separatism of any brand, the tireless men and women workers for civil rights and peace.

What then ails the "revolution"? Above all, it is that we are not sure who is in control, and the leaders of the "revolution", within government and without, do not seem to know either. The Honourable René Lévesque's call to the young people of Quebec to place their trust in democracy, rather than in violence, and to beware of oversimplifications (before the Quebec City Chamber of Commerce, March 19, 1964) betokens concern within Provincial Government circles lest the initiative slip from their grasp. Affirmations from the Liberal Ministry of Quebec that they represent *all* the citizens of the Province — not just those of "French" origin — are badly needed now. Firm leadership on the part of our Government would serve to remind extremists that they have been invoking false analogies; that they have overemphasized the notion of nationality to the detriment of humanity; that they are in process of becoming a "language bloc" with a peculiar outlook on the world that is biased and inflexible.

This is Hugh Myers' first book. When you have read it, I suspect

---

* In this connection see André Morel, "L'histoire de la confessionalité scolaire au Québec", in *Justice et paix scolaire*, Preface by Jacques Mackay, Editions du Jour, Montreal, 1962, and C. B. Sissons, *Church and State in Canadian Education: an Historical View*, Ryerson, Toronto, 1959. The presumed right of separate denominational schools to state support under our constitution appears to be in conflict with a more basic right. That is, the right of the individual (a freeman) to enjoy the full protection of the constitution as a member of the community (the town meeting) rather than as a member of a religious congregation alone.

that you will agree with Mr. Dooley* who said:

"When a man has something to say and don't know how to say it, he says it pretty well."

Maynard Gertler.

Montreal
March 20, 1964

---

* Peter Finley Dunne.

AUTHOR'S PROLOGUE

What do I really mean by the "revolution"? Essentially, the idea is that in 1958 or 1959 (I call 1958 pre-revolutionary, but won't quibble), a reaction against the Establishment, as the British call it, became too strong to be ignored. For all the separatist noises, this reaction was and is *equally* against the established French Canadian, Quebec order of things. Day by day this force has become more irresistible in its power. Always the cry is for justice, or at least for something — anything — rather than the *status quo;* always the protest is against injustice on the part of those in high places. Whether the alleged injustices are largely real or not is another matter, but *the Province is ever more inclined to believe, as time goes on, that the denunciations of perfidy we hear are indeed correct, true to fact.* With each passing day, the protests of the firebrand few get ever more extreme, public receptivity and support towards them increases, and time contracts as one upset of the old system is piled upon another.

Quebec must be chaos and lunacy to anyone who does not either more or less hold the above view or entertain another global theory that accounts for the facts. I am not dogmatic, but let us look at the Coffin case. In 1958, two years after Coffin's execution, Hébert brought out *Coffin était innocent.* It caused a small stir and was forgotten. Now, when the whole affair should be remote history, he returns to the attack and sweeps all before him.

On the face of it, what sense does it make? A *Devoir* cartoon showing a female bear worrying her hibernating mate with something like "If I were you I wouldn't sleep so unconcernedly; they're still looking for the murderers of those Americans!" seems as apt a comment as any.

It makes sense if you accept the revolution as a fact. In 1958, the public couldn't get excited over a case which was, it seemed, over and done with. Now it is passionately interested in that same case because, after four or five years of the revolution, of extreme protest against authority, IT IS READY TO BELIEVE A MAN WHO ACCUSES PROVINCIAL AUTHORITIES OF LEGAL MURDER. With their new awareness, the people sense that if one man can be strung up that way, so can ten, a hundred, or a thousand men.

In 1958, *Le Devoir* threw everything into an attack on the government; it represented some ministers as swindlers. It never really got the public with it, not for a year or two anyway. Now ONE MAN calls down some of our most mighty judges and policemen, saying they're just a lot of assassins, and receives such a wave of instant, spontaneous support that in less than a month (the book appeared on December 11) the government has to do just what he says it should do, that is, set up a Royal Commission to investigate the conduct of the Coffin trial and the behaviour of all concerned.

PREFACE

As the year 1963 began, Canadians were growing used to comment about Quebec's "quiet revolution". Because of its separatist overtones, many people felt that it was something one should know about, like the dangers of fall-out or of cigarette smoking. Like them it was vaguely disquieting or even menacing; like them it evoked grave warnings from solemn people, such as Frank Willis on *Close-Up*. Like them, too, it obliged no one to take any action, and like them it offered to a complacent society the hope that it might never make much difference in one's day-to-day routine if only people didn't get too excited about it — that is, if only they didn't really *do* anything about it.

Then, on March 8, three of Her Majesty's military establishments in Montreal were the targets of Molotov cocktails. In the weeks that followed, the Wolfe monument on the Plains of Abraham in Quebec City was sent crashing to the ground; a railway track that the Prime Minister (Mr. Diefenbaker) was to pass over was dynamited; an R.C.M.P. building was damaged by a bomb; another bomb, exploding behind one of Her Majesty's recruiting centers, killed the night watchman; a Black Watch depot was bombed; an explosion occurred in an oil refinery; five mail boxes blew up in the rich, largely English, Montreal suburb of Westmount; a sergeant-major, about to dismantle a mail box bomb, was nearly killed by it; a bomb exploded in an engineering building; dynamite was found in Quebec City mail boxes.

There was a lull. The Premier of the State (for it was no longer wholly acceptable to refer to it as a province, or even as a Province), although securely in office until at least 1966, barring assassination or acts of God, showed signs of perturbation and went so far as to offer $50,000.00 to any public-spirited citizen willing to provide information leading to the apprehension and conviction of those responsible. (Compare this with the paltry sum that used to be offered for telling on someone who did wilfully damage Her Majesty's railway coach. CN's Quebec City investigations department informs us that the practice of posting reward signs in passenger cars was discontinued some time ago. It tended to incite certain persons to make unfounded charges and claims, and many people felt the railway was responsible for its own policing and shouldn't have to rely on the public for help.) Clearly, the FLQ was something that could interfere with such things as foreign investment, good-will tours to Great Britain, and perhaps even the tourist industry. At last, even the police showed signs of concern. All available suspects were rounded up. Many French Canadians had the impression that they were found guilty without trial or defense at a coroner's inquest, and another historic blunder was on the books. Now one could have a good cry over the way the nasty policemen had treated *"les bons petits terroristes de chez-nous"*.

When Canada's Grey Cup football game reaches half-time, there is always a few minutes' pause while the players rest, the majorettes march, and the spectators talk about what has happened so far, speculate on the why and how of it all, and try to guess how the match will turn out. Without stretching comparisons, the Grey Cup event and the Quebec revolution have in common at least their feverish struggles, heated passions, burning pursuits of absolute victory, and fascinated spectators. As one of the latter, the author invites other observers, as well as those who have been unable to follow Quebec's action-packed drama as closely as they might have wished, to take a little time out to review, and if possible to clarify, our ideas about what has occurred, and what it all means. People who speak mostly French, people who have played and are playing major or minor roles in the kaleidoscopic scenes of Quebec, people that the author meets and talks with every day in the streets of Quebec City — these together with the headlines, stories, editorials, and letter columns of French-language newspapers are to be our first sources. When a book makes the news, it too will have to receive our attention, for in a book a revolution may describe itself.

When did the revolution begin? Since it began so quietly, is it possible for us to select one day in particular, and to describe everything before this as the Old Province, everything after it as the New State? Mr. André Laurendeau, editor-in-chief of the Montreal daily *Le Devoir* and co-chairman of the Royal Commission on Biculturalism, whom the author regards as one of French Canada's principal unofficial spokesmen, may help us here. Quoted below are the opening paragraphs from his leading article, entitled "Quebec, Year IV", in the fifteen-page supplement on the economic future of the province — I mean, State — to be found in *Le Devoir* of June 22, 1963:

"Year IV, and not at all Year III: the new epoch began in September, 1959, with the death of Somebody.

"The historian will be better able to show us the causes and connections. But it is necessary to record that rupture — the explosion.

"Must we go back further, and regard as a direct precursor the federal election of March 1958? Quebec, having lost one of its two kings — the most distant, suzerain rather than autocrat, the federal Liberal leader Louis St. Laurent — manifested its new availability by supporting Diefenbaker. We believed at the time that Quebec was flying to the aid of the victor, and it is true that, far down in its social strata, with its pauper's habits, the province loves power, which it believes it needs. Yet was there not something revolutionary in this sudden support, without love for Diefenbaker or any of his lieutenants (if indeed he had any), of a party that we have rejected since Laurier?

"For the rest, this return of the Conservatives to Ottawa will have fortunate consequences: by his great disdain for the highly-placed administrator and for the intellectual, Diefenbaker will later aid, without wishing it, the provincial Liberals to repatriate a number of young representatives of the civil service, and to mobilize the intelligentsia for Quebec.

"But the psychological revolution begins with Paul Sauvé.

"In three weeks he made it clear that his government did not resemble that of his predecessor and ex-chief. From now on, intelligent suggestions would not be automatically dismissed, nor their authors insulted. It was under him that education began to be looked on with real interest. Thanks to statutory grants, arbitrary methods of aid received a setback. The province, stiff-jointed, undertook to unfold and stretch itself: what joy and what hope, yet in an element still calm."

As André Laurendeau indicates, the death of "Somebody" (Maurice Duplessis) gives a logical point of departure for the revolutionary calendar. As he also indicates, a good look at 1958 may be well worth our while, and it is with that year, the pre-revolutionary year, that our chronology begins.

CHAPTER ONE
1958

OUR ONLY MAJOR GRIEVANCE

The revolution has many aspects. There have been, and are now, a multitude of radical new projects brought to light to revolutionize education in the province. There have been, and are now, an impressive number of ambitious schemes in progress or in preparation to give French Canadians greater control over the vast natural wealth of their province, to give them more of the key positions, and thus to make them richer, more powerful, more independent of the English-speaking continent that, north of Mexico, surrounds them. There have been, and there are now, urgent struggles on the part of French Canadians in Quebec to obtain redress of old grievances from English Canadians, and to be at least equal to them in all respects, particularly in dignity and in opportunity for advancement.

Since resentment against English Canada has recently reached the point at which death and injury can result, let us see how English Canada is presented in *Le Devoir* of 1958.

"Simultaneous translation is *very good*. Bilingual cheques *would be* much better."

So reads the title of the major *Le Devoir* editorial for February 11, 1958. The emphasis is the paper's. In the body of the article, which is signed by Pierre Vigeant, we find that "The cheques printed by the government represent our only major grievance."

English Canadians who read Mr. Vigeant's editorial must have thought that, after all, French-Canadian Quebec is not very hard to satisfy. "Our only major grievance" could obviously have been removed in a day, with no trouble at all. Moreover, Mr. Vigeant quite definitely takes an optimistic view of life when, in an editorial dated December 30, he unhesitatingly and boldy affirms that "English-Canadian opinion has shown itself to be more and more favourable towards bilingualism during the last few years". Once again, however, Mr. Vigeant feels it needful to bring the question of bilingual cheques to the fore. A part of the editorial deals with

1

a bill in their favour that has, at this time, been brought before the Commons by Mr. Louis Joseph Pigeon. Vigeant feels assured that the measure will pass easily. His thinking on the matter shows little or no change since the beginning of the year as he writes that the absence of such cheques represents "the worst deficiency in the observance of official bilingualism".

Give French Canada bilingual cheques, seems to be the message of 1958, and even the militantly nationalist newspaper founded by the great Henri Bourassa in 1910, and ever since renowned for its unrelenting defense of his people's rights, will at last be satisfied, and everyone will be able to live happily ever afterwards, in brotherly love and good fellowship.

Would French Canada, at least the Quebec part of it, really have been so easily satisfied? We'll never know. Perhaps for a time. Perhaps many French Canadians, like Mr. Vigeant, would have thought that, after all, the English are phlegmatic by temperament; that you can't expect them to do anything quickly or respond to more than one request at a time. Perhaps they would have thought that such matters as greater French-Canadian participation in the upper echelons of the federal civil service and crown corporations, together with more bilingualism in these areas, and greater respect for bilingualism and biculturalism in the other provinces, could be dealt with later, one by one. Perhaps their revolution, when it came, would have been less hostile and demanding towards English Canada.

We'll never know. They didn't get bilingual cheques, not then, not when it seemed to count. To say that when, a little over three years later, they finally did get them, they were not satisfied, would be the understatement of any century.

The author was in Quebec City in the summer of 1958, studying French at Laval University, and was thus afforded the opportunity of questioning some of the professors about the relationships between French and English Canada. In general, they felt that things were getting better.

THE NATURAL GAS SCANDAL

In the summer of 1958, *Le Devoir* launched what can only be described as a full-scale offensive against the Union Nationale government. If the *"Scandale du gaz naturel"*, as the paper called it, did not immediately precipitate the revolution, it must surely have done much to pave the way for it, for no revolution can get started until the existing scheme of things has been thoroughly discredited* The object of this journalistic campaign was to prove that the cabinet of Premier Maurice Duplessis contained a disquieting number of honourable swindlers.

The paper began to draw up its forces early in the year. On February 8, Mr. Gérard Filion, then its Editor, now head of the Liberal government's General Investment Corporation, described the Natural Gas Corporation of Quebec as "one of the numerous bastard children of Mr. Maurice Duplessis." May 13, saw "Gas, a Swindle" as the title of the major editorial by Pierre Vigeant. The government-owned Hydro-Quebec, he asserted, had sold its natural gas system to the Corporation, which was now proceeding to make excessive profits out of it by charging too much. Mr. Vigeant's solution: nationalize the gas company.

Editorials by the same writer and on the same theme appeared on May 19, 22, 26 and 30. All this we may consider as the preparation, the softening-up. It continued on June 4 and 9.

On Friday, June 13, *Le Devoir* went to war; and if there are Union Nationale members who shudder at the thought of Friday the thirteenth, any Friday the thirteenth, it would hardly be fair to accuse them of superstition. *Le Devoir*, which normally keeps to conservative black, not too large headlines, came out with a great, screaming, blood-red banner that needs no translation:

Scandale à la Corporation de Gas Naturel de Québec

The accusation was that at least six ministers, and possibly Duplessis himself, had speculated in Natural Gas Corporation stocks, the value of which had been increased through the government's sale of gas rights to the corporation.

Saturday, June 14: Double red banner headlines surrounded by the names and photographs of the six ministers accused. All of the front page given over to the affair. The editorial by Gérard Filion calls for the resignation of the ministers.

Monday, June 16: Red banner headline. Photographs of Duplessis and Jean Lesage. All of the front page given over to the affair.

* "Mass movements do not usually arise until the prevailing order has been discredited. The discrediting is not an automatic result of the blunders and abuses of those in power, but the deliberate work of men of words with a grievance. Where the articulate are absent or without a grievance, the prevailing dispensation, though incompetent and corrupt, may continue in power until it falls and crumbles of itself. On the other hand, a dispensation of undoubted merit and vigor may be swept away if it fails to win the allegiance of the articulate minority." Eric Hoffer, *The True Believer*, New York, The New American Library, 1958, p. 119.

And so it goes. For the rest of the summer, until the beginning of August at least, *Le Devoir* will continue to hammer away with everything it has. Headlines, frequently red, on "*Le Scandale*" will appear almost every day. The big guns of Gérard Filion will lay down much of the accompanying editorial barrage. After the mid-summer onslaught is over, stories and editorials on the subject will continue to appear, at intervals, not only in 1958, but in the coming years of the revolution. A large part of the Liberal campaign of 1960 will be based upon promises to give the province honest government, and to investigate the Union Nationale administration in general, and its natural gas dealings in particular.

As this was being written, the Salvas Commission, appointed by the Lesage cabinet to investigate Union Nationale administration, made a report on the alleged thousands of dollars paid in *patronage* by government contractors of the Duplessis days, and condemned a number of major *Union* figures whom it did not fear to name.

THE NEGRO KING

While *Le Devoir* (French Canadian) assaulted the Union Nationale (French Canadian), there may have been a number of English Canadians who sat back comfortably to watch, happy to be left out of it all. If so, these individuals, or at least those among them who read *Le Devoir*, may have received some enlightenment as their well-cushioned armchairs were subjected, with no advance warning whatever, to the full lethal jolt of Mr. André Laurendeau's "*roi nègre*" (Negro King) editorial of July 4.

A few days previously, Mr. Duplessis, having decided in the course of a press conference that he could no longer tolerate the presence of *Devoir* reporter Guy Lamarche, had at first told him to leave, and, this failing, had then had him ejected by the police. While *Le Devoir* had of course protested as vigorously as it could, and had been backed up staunchly by the other major French-language newspapers of the province, the English-language press had said little or nothing about the matter. As a result we have the theory of the "Negro King", the essential features of which we must now examine.

"Usually," Mr. Laurendeau writes, "the English are more sensitive than we are to infringements of all forms of liberty. This is why Mr. Duplessis has a bad press outside of Quebec."

In this, prejudice plays some part but "We would be wrong to explain everything by ethnic prejudices. The British conquered their political liberties a little at a time. They know their price that much better, and they are usually more alert to threats against them."

If Ottawa tries to muzzle free discussion, all the English papers complain that liberty has been violated. Witness the pipeline affair. Yet, "In the Legislative Assembly of Quebec, incidents of that type occur every day. Our English papers take them with hardly a murmur. Why?"

Mr. Laurendeau then affirms that neither the *Montreal Star* nor the *Gazette* really protested the Lamarche incident. He goes on:

"Quebec's Anglophones behave like the British in one of their African colonies.

"The British are too wise, politically; they rarely destroy the political institutions of a conquered country. They surround the Negro King, but they let him behave as he pleases. Occasionally he will be permitted to cut off heads if it's customary. It would never occur to them to demand of a Negro King that he conform to the high moral and political standards of the British.

"The Negro King must collaborate and protect the interests of the British. With this taken care of, the rest counts for little. Does the little king violate the rules of democracy? Well, what could one expect from such a primitive creature?

"I don't attribute these attitudes to the English minority of Quebec. But things happen as though some of its leaders believed in the theory and practice of the Negro King. They pardon in Mr. Duplessis, chief of Quebec's natives, what they wouldn't stand for in one of their own.

"One sees it daily in the Legislative Assembly. It was evident in the last municipal election. It has just been verified at Quebec.

"As a result, democracy and parliamentary practice regress, and arbitrary rule goes uncontested. There is constant collusion between Anglo-Quebec finance and everything that is the most rotten in the politics of this province."

How can you be surprised that some of us are separatists, the French Canadian sometimes asks his English-speaking neighbour, when we can never depend upon you? You argue that we are stronger together than we would be separated. But at best you are fair-weather friends. What you try to market as realism and efficiency is really a cold expediency that never knew the name of loyalty, of truth, or of honour. If ever we get into trouble, if ever we are faced with a situation that is too much for us to handle alone, we can never look to you for support. Bitter experience has taught us that you will throw us over without a second's thought when your own selfish interests can be served thereby.

From this time on, French Canadians in general, and separatists in particular, will be able to use the name of André Laurendeau when they wish to argue that Quebec is held in tutelage by English Canada, that it is no better off than the lowliest Imperial fief.

While the Lamarche incident provided the occasion for the Negro King editorial, Mr. Laurendeau's thought here had no doubt evolved over a period of years. Mr. Duplessis' gesture in expelling the reporter was, after all, only a gesture. It was too late for the Premier to have any serious thought of actually suppressing Le Devoir unless he could muster the strength to shatter its Natural Gas onslaught with a potent counter offensive.

Apparently he could not.

THE DIEFENBAKER LANDSLIDE

1958 was the year in which the Progressive Conservatives won a federal election with the biggest majority in Canadian history. As we have seen, Mr. Laurendeau wonders if there was not something revolutionary in the fact that this massive support included Quebec. Mr. Laurendeau's views, as always, merit the most careful consideration, and it is true that the revolution has in it an element of desperation that makes Quebec more unpredictable than before. It will try anything once. Nevertheless, as it is scarcely credible that the Quebec we now know would vote heavily Conservative, the election results of March 31, 1958, may also be taken as an indication that the revolution had yet to begin.

By their victory, the ill-starred Conservatives assured themselves of being in office to face the wrath of the new Quebec, which lost no time in recapitulating the long list of situations it wouldn't stand for any longer and in discovering many new ones. To impatient French Canadians, Ottawa would appear mainly to stall, obstruct, and obfuscate when confronted with their exigencies. Mackenzie King had left to those who were to succeed him the sublime memory of how the art of waitmanship, or the policy of delay and stay put, could with assiduous application and unflinching adherence to the seat of one's chair, be exalted to a degree of superlative perfection. He could not, alas, bequeath to them his brains.

POPE JOHN XXIII

Before the election of Pope John XXIII in 1958, there were doubtless many Quebecers who felt that to be in favour of change, let alone revolution, was to set oneself against the Church itself. With the new Pope came new and farther horizons. Heaven itself seemed to become more spacious, more accommodating. "In My Father's house there are many mansions."

"In spite of his farmbred love of land and custom, John XXIII was, in the best possible sense, a revolutionary — a Pope of modernization who kept in continuity with the past, yet made even the most enlightened of his twentieth century predecessors seem like voices from another age."*

---

* *Time*, June 7, 1963.

CHAPTER TWO
1959

Although 1959 is the year in which the revolution begins, the impression to be gleaned from the pages of *Le Devoir* does not always reflect this fact. At times, indeed, it is quite reassuring to English Canada. Thus, on page 3 of the April 8 issue, we find Mr. Michel Chartrand, one-time leader of the province's Social Democratic Party (CCF) and now President of the Socialist Party of Quebec, impressed by the vogue for French in the West, a vogue which, he says, is becoming greater and greater. He notes the increasing desire of English Canadians to know French.

On page 12, *Le Devoir* of February 15 reports that the February 14 *Maclean's* favours more bilingualism in the civil service.

In a front page *Devoir* article on Manitoba (May 22) Pierre Laporte° is happy to acknowledge that in forty years "the recognition of the rights of the French language has risen from zero to nearly one hundred percent". In 1916 the government abolished the right to teach French, but since then progress in the opposite direction has been such that "French has greater and greater liberty in Manitoba" and it "is no longer tolerated but accepted."

Two more front-page articles on the same subject and by the same writer complete the series. In the second, he is rather worried about the future of French in Manitoba because "the necessity to fight for the recognition of French no longer existing, it is feared that the ability of the young to resist may wither away". Highly significant also is Mr. Laporte's contention, in the third article, that it is Quebec's own fault if it is little known in Manitoba.

Gérard Filion, in his September 12 editorial, affirms that "there presently exists in Canada a climate favourable to French-Canadian culture." Also in September Governor-General Vanier, the first French Canadian ever nominated to represent the British Sovereign in Canada, takes office.

° The present Minister of Municipal Affairs in the Province of Quebec who is also a well-known journalist and author.

Yet, despite the evenness of temper, all is not sweetness and light. On May 12, a *Devoir* editorial by Pierre Vigeant underlines once again French Canada's resistance to any measure that might cause it to lose its identity in the Canadian melting-pot. For the 1961 census, the government proposes to include "Canadian" among the possible answers to the question about ethnic background, and Mr. Vigeant is concerned lest the number of French Canadians that exists be lost in this answer. Notably, he suspects that the census-takers may contrive to popularize the answer, to get as many "Canadians" as possible. As the census nears and the revolution develops, this issue will become explosive; for the time being it can wait and the tone of the editorial is moderate.

Much more serious with respect to 1959 and to the anti-English turn that the revolution takes, is the C.B.C. strike to be dealt with in the following section. Also a report by Alberta's Cameron Commission on Education does Canadian unity little good. "Too Much French In Alberta" is the title of the major Gérard Filion editorial of November 18, 1959. With bitter irony he goes on to recognize that "an hour (of French) a day from Grades 3 to 6 is a waste of time", for the Cameron Commission has just recommended that it be halved. With its piercing intellect, the Commission has discovered that French is just another language. Mr. Filion, after presenting the usual counter-arguments, sums it all up with: "If the stupid obstinacy of the majority does not permit them (the French Canadians) to flourish throughout Canada, they will fall back on the Province of Quebec."

Separatist trumpets shrilled loud and clear in the fall of 1959 as the revolution got under way. The Cameron Commission report came just at the right time to help the separatists get started as they developed their argument that French Canadians enjoy the full rights of citizenship only in Quebec.

THE SHOW MUST NOT GO ON

"Before the strike," said Mr. Jean Pelletier, "there was just one union for both French and English-speaking authors and artists. It was *The Canadian Conference of Authors and Artists,* or CCAA.

"The strike was what set the whole thing on fire. It caused a complete break. Now the CCAA represents only English-speaking Canadians. The new French Canadian union, of which I am one of the board of directors, is called *La Fédération des auteurs et des artistes du Canada,* or FAAC. An agreement was made between the Federation and the CBC on July 12, 1963. The CCAA and the FAAC had officially separated shortly before that."

Our informant works in the Provincial Secretary's Department in Quebec. More to the point for purposes of the present discussion, he is also a free-lance performer on CBC radio and television, is on the board of the new Federation as we have seen, and is similarly on the board of *La Société des artistes de Québec* (Quebec Artists' Society), which is affiliated with the Federation. Equally affiliated with the Federation is the *Union des artistes de Montréal* (Montreal Artists' Union).

It is doubtful whether anything since World War II and conscription has caused more sense of grievance among French Canadians than the strike in question. From December 29, 1958, until March 7, 1959, it paralysed the whole of the French language network of the CBC*, with what bitter results we shall see in the pages to follow.

"When the strike started," Mr. Pelletier continued, "the Montreal Artists' Union, at that time associated with the CCAA, decided to back the producers. (The producers, you will remember, were the ones directly involved who sparked the strike because the CBC refused to recognize their right to form a union). But the head office of the CCAA in Toronto condemned the initiative of the Montreal Artists' Union, which was told that it should mind its own business and let the producers fight their own battles. Naturally, the Montreal union resented such censure from Toronto.

"So after the strike, it decided to withdraw from the CCAA. The Quebec Artists' Union, which had also been associated with the CCAA, followed suit, and the two joined forces to create the Federation we now have.

"The CCAA resisted the separation as strongly as it could, but to no avail. As I have said, the Federation officially parted company with it this year.

"Mr. René Lévesque, incidentally, was very influential in the whole strike scene."

What, then, are the salient details of the terrible strike? It started with seventy-four *Radio Canada* producers. It stuck because some three thousand of their fellow workers observed their picket lines, and indeed added to their effectiveness, in the sub-zero depths of a

---

* "The title Canadian Broadcasting Corporation or *Radio Canada* in French, covers the total operation of the CBC." See Albert A. Shea, *Broadcasting: The Canadian Way*, Harvest House, Montreal, 1963.

Quebec winter, for seventy days, with never a pay-cheque to warm the heart and send the blood coursing through numb extremities. It is led by Jean Marchand. Throughout its duration it is front-page news in *Le Devoir*. While it is difficult to arrive at a single, over-all impression, it is clear that, in general, things go from bad to worse.

On December 31, *Le Devoir* reports that Toronto refuses to do the Montreal program "The Concert Hour". Presumably, Toronto thus earns at least a little approval from *les artistes*.

January 5, news is bad: *Radio Canada* is reported to have demanded a return to work.

On January 7, Mr. André Laurendeau protests *Radio Canada's* special bulletin, ordering the strikers back to work.

On January 9, the producers are reported to have appealed to Prime Minister Diefenbaker and Labour Minister Starr to intervene. The following day we learn that Mr. Starr has refused on technical grounds.

January 13, sees a "hardening" on both sides.

On January 22, Mr. Laurendeau writes a front-page editorial blaming *Radio Canada* for its rigidity and calling for federal action.

January 26, however, brings the encouraging news that Montreal is supported by its Toronto comrades.

But on January 27, fifteen strikers march on Ottawa.

On February 7, the opposition in the House of Commons attacks government do-nothing-ness, and on February 20, *Le Devoir* announces that things are completely deadlocked.

On March 1, just when everything seems settled at last, *Radio Canada* reneges on an agreement made three weeks previously.

The explosion finally comes. On March 3, *Le Devoir* reports demonstrations of one thousand strikers outside *Radio Canada's* Dorchester Boulevard building. Hundreds of police, some of them mounted, had allegedly entered the fray, and twenty-eight strikers had been locked up.

There are two memorable pictures on page one. One of them shows Mr. René Lévesque, then a member of the Montreal Artists' Union, now Quebec's Minister of Natural Resources and the great driving force in the government, being led, very peacefully, into a police wagon. The second picture shows Mr. Lévesque, still very calm, being released.

In an article entitled *"Radio Canada* is a Fiction; The Reality is called 'C.B.C.' "*, which the March 7 *Devoir* carries on page two, Mr. Lévesque presents his view of the situation.

"It has lasted sixty-eight days today," begins Mr. Lévesque, writing as usual in French. "A month ago today, exactly, *Radio Canada* signed an agreement which it was bound to respect. It will be a week ago tomorrow since *Radio Canada* refused to honour its word, thus in front of everyone transforming a strike which was already very harsh into a lockout which makes of this crown corporation an indescribable public starver. All through these sixty-eight days, moving noiselessly beside bad faith and crashing ultimatums, supporting with its impalpable presence (and with taxpayers' money) the brutal irresponsibility of a few great and small administrators, there has also been something more, something nearly intangible and at the same time monstrous, which refuses obstinately to show its true face. Moreover, it's a face that would try desperately to grimace a smile if perchance one managed to unmask it. The rest of this article is written in the language that this face speaks. Coldly, I believe, with no other feeling than that of the accumulated weariness of two months of holding back and disillusionment."

Mr. Lévesque writes the rest of his article in English.

Following is a list of the strikers' chief targets:

The Montreal Star, which is accused of giving a false, biased account of the March 3 demonstration, blaming the strikers instead of the police.

The Montreal Gazette, said to be even worse.

The CBC's chief negotiators, who are accused of being mainly English. Bruce Raymond, Clive McKee, and Ron Fraser are mentioned.

The House of Commons (mainly English) which has "The final authority over public radio and television."

Labour Minister Starr, who refuses to intervene even though (Mr. Lévesque says) it's his duty.

National Revenue Minister George Nowlan, who has termed the strike "illegal".

Prime Minister Diefenbaker, who has refused to act.

Much is made of the fact that all three of the last-mentioned are English.

One passage deals with French Canada's pride in its public affairs programs, its *"Télé-théâtre"*, and its nationally-broadcast Concert Hour.

"CBC's higher-ups have run the gamut from corporate irresponsibility to anonymous viciousness."

Cabinet ministers are accused of "denseness, small-town vanity and brutal indifference."

Winding it all up, Mr. Lévesque concludes with the following words:

"Some of us, maybe a lot of us, will come out of this permanently disgusted with a certain ideal called National Unity. Never before have we felt that, apart from pleas every four years in painful "Political French", National Unity is something designed almost exclusively to keep negligible minorities nice and quiet.

"Never before have we felt that our affairs are bound to be either tragically or comically mismanaged, as long as they remain in the hands of men who have no understanding of them, and make it quite clear that they don't consider such lack as any kind of a personal flaw.

"Some of us, and maybe many, come out of this with a tired and unworthy feeling that if such a strike had happened on the English CBC, it would — as the Hon. George Nowlan said, on this occasion not erroneously — have lasted no more than half an hour. To this day, ours has lasted sixty-eight days. Of such signal advantages is the privilege of being French made up in this country!

"And even at the risk of being termed 'horrid nationalists', we feel that at least once before the conflict is over, we have to make plain our deep appreciation of such an enviable place in the great bilingual, bicultural, and fraternal Canadian sun. . . ."

On the day the above was published, the strike ended in victory for the producers.

In his March 11, *Devoir* editorial, Gérard Filion sums up the Lévesque position, but also mentions a few counter-arguments:

"The chief negotiator of the Corporation was a French Canadian; the local management in Montreal against which the strike was directed was wholly French Canadian; the attitude of some of Quebec's Conservative Members of Parliament was as mean as it could be."

At times one feels that French Canadians are prejudiced against themselves.

Nevertheless, and for the future most significant:

"There have been some funny conversions during these last two months. Our writers and artists are generally those who used to turn up their noses at . . . French-Canadian nationalism . . . And yet, since the beginning of January, we've seen more nationalist slogans on the strikers' picket lines and in their meetings than at any other time or place in French Canada."

And Mr. Filion suggests that French-Canadian nationalism may be just a reaction to hostility or lack of understanding from the majority.

The author of this book felt that his present study of the matter would not be complete without an interview with the powerful Minister who was so deeply involved in it. Mr. Lévesque was kind enough to receive me on November 6, 1963. Following is an account of relevant parts of the interview.

"Mr. Lévesque, what was your principal means of livelihood at the time of the strike?"

"A program called *Point de mire* — Focus, I guess, is what you might call it in English. I was a free-lance, but this *Radio Canada* program kept me busy for fifty to sixty hours a week and gave me my basic income. I liked it very much. The idea was to report and comment upon a topic taken from a current news headline."

"After more than two months of strike, you wrote an article saying that there was no *Radio Canada,* just the CBC. Is the situation still the same?

"I've been out of it for four years now. It's hard to say. I don't suppose anything has really changed. Our attitude sprang from the fact that you really felt like a minority, sometimes like a minority without even a voice.

"The whole French network was closed down. About three thousand people were out of work. A lot of them were getting pretty desperate.

"Forty-eight hours of such a strike on the English network would have panicked them in Ottawa. After more than two months of it on our network, a lot of people were hungry. But it didn't seem to disturb the gentlemen.

"You couldn't reason with anyone; no one would listen. You had to use sticks and stones to impress anyone.

"Apparently they thought they'd just starve us till we gave up.

"It made me feel what it means to be a minority when you don't have the strength to force the majority to pay attention to you. I felt that we were accounted negligible, and that if ever our chance came to be less negligible, we should use it. I realized, too, that any action in this sense would have to be political.

"Four years in the government hasn't made me less skeptical

about Canada. I know Quebec is my country. I'm not quite convinced that Canada is."

Mr. Lévesque paused. "I suppose the Ottawa of 1963, with policies you see as intrusive and centralizing, doesn't seem too enlightened," I ventured, forgetting for a minute about the strike.

"Even if nothing else were involved, decentralization makes economic sense. In British Columbia, Mr. Bennett doesn't hesitate to get up on one of his mountains and tell Ottawa to keep its distance. And yet he has only provincial interests to defend. He is English, just as is Ottawa. Here we have a double responsibility: provincial interests and French Canada.

"I cannot picture myself as Mr. Bishop. I am at home in French. I am French. But if you are to be French, you have to have a place you can call your own.

"We don't try to tell the other provinces what to do. All we want is the right to act in Quebec, where we are at home, without finding federal roadblocks everywhere.

"The federal government is incompetent enough in its own domain. Take defense — look at the hash they make of it. Why can't they learn to do their own job instead of meddling with us?"

"Would you nevertheless prefer to stay in Confederation?" I asked.

"Yes, but not on the condition of having the dice loaded against us. And they still are."

Here Mr. Lévesque came over with the day's issue of *La Presse*, Montreal's big French daily, and put his finger on an item.

"You understand French, don't you? Try to imagine that you are French Canadian for a minute. How do you expect us to be happy in Confederation when one still reads such things?"

The story said that on October 15, a certain Mr. Bates, President of the Central Housing and Mortgage Corporation, had boasted that he had successfully resisted pressures from French-speaking federal ministers in favour of having a French Canadian named as either vice-president or member of the board. On this occasion, Mr. Bates had been announcing the appointment of two English Canadians to these posts.

"How would you feel," asked the Minister, "if the president of a crown corporation could make that boast with respect to your people?"

He pointed back to the article. "Now, at last, after who knows how many complaints and interventions, Mr. Bates finds it possible to appoint Mr. St-Pierre and Mr. Lupien to the board. And to do that he has to raise the number of board members from four to six!

"And look at what we had to go through to get recognition in the CNR. And look at the other crown corporations in which we are restricted to a minor role.

"They talk about our educational system. Yet often we have many men available with the same academic background as many highly-placed English Canadians. Look at the lawyers — I don't know how many lawyers we've got. As to quality, brains, and achievement, we don't notice that English Canadians are exactly world-beaters!

"Do we have to stage a demonstration, a march on Ottawa every time we want a little justice?

"Either we are Canadians or we're not. Either we have rights or we don't. If we don't, we'd better stop pretending."

"Mr. Lévesque, did you enter politics because of the strike?"

"It was a factor. But I wouldn't say just the strike, no. There was much else. I suppose the long years of Duplessis had something to do with it."

"Exactly when did you join the Liberals?"

"At the beginning of May, 1960, when I agreed to run in the election. Just a month and a half before the election itself. Before that I wasn't a member of any party."

As I left, I felt that this last bit of information was significant. The Minister was still a political critic at heart, not a politician.

There is a difference.

Yet must one not think carefully before withholding one's vote from a man who, so obviously, is not seeking it?

In the late summer of this year (1963), the whole ugly strike situation was brought back to French-Canadian minds by the dispute between the Montreal Artists' Union and the American-controlled Actors' Equity, both of which claimed, and still claim, union rights over the spectacular new Montreal concert hall, *Place des Arts.*

Once again the Montreal union felt itself isolated and helpless except for its sister union, the Quebec Artists' Society and sympathetic French-Canadian opinion. In 1959, according to André Laurendeau in the *Devoir* of August 31, 1963, the Montreal unions felt themselves "poorly supported or even abandoned" by Toronto, and thus similarly isolated.

Once again there was an unhealthy state of inaction, a lack of anyone willing and able to decide. Yet perhaps the worst was averted, at least for the time being, when the Montreal union and Actors' Equity came to a truce shortly before the Concert Hall's September 21 opening. It was too late for *les artistes* to change their mind about not participating, and first-nighters were treated to a concert instead of the varied festival originally planned. But at least the Montreal Artists did not stage a demonstration. The separatists, however, were there in their place to recall March 3, 1959, and once again the police, some of them mounted, moved in. Once again, some people went to jail.

It is likely that no one with the capacities of the Honourable René Lévesque was directly involved.

THE WORK AND THE WORKERS

"For us, it all started with the Asbestos strike of 1949. It brought the fundamental problems of the province to light by showing the link between the *Union Nationale* government and international finance. For here was the paradox: Duplessis, head of a nationalist government, was supporting the American-owned Canadian Johns-Manville Company against a French-Canadian union, affiliated with the Confederation of Catholic Workers of Canada.

"The strike involved the Church, which favoured us, and all French-Canadian institutions. They were usually on our side too. It was the beginning of the end for Duplessis. His position then weakened. He was no longer able to be a dictator."

The speaker was Mr. Jean Marchand, President of the Confederation of National Trade Unions and a resident of Quebec City. Marchand, a very youthful man of 46 years, studied at the Commercial Academy of Quebec and Laval University's School of Social Sciences before joining the labour movement in 1942 as an organizer of the National Federation of Pulp and Paper Workers.

He became an organizer of the Confederation in 1944, its general secretary in 1947, and its president in 1961. The Confederation of National Trade Unions used to be the Confederation of Catholic Workers of Canada, but changed its name in 1961 when it decided not to be exclusively Catholic.

"The province exploded," said Jean Marchand, "with the death of Duplessis. Before he died, the only ones to oppose him openly were *Le Devoir, Cité Libre,* and the Confederation of Catholic Workers of Canada, as we were then called."

During our talk (late 1963), Jean Marchand, now a member of the Royal Commission on Biculturalism, affirmed that Mr. Duplessis exploited nationalist feeling but never really did anything to promote the economic interests of French Canadians. He was cynical and knew what he was doing.

"If he had been really interested in French Canadians he would have reformed the educational system and aided the province's economic life."

Asbestos is a mining town in the Eastern Townships, close to the American border. The strike in question, described in Herbert F. Quinn's recent book *The Union Nationale*, took on, before it ended, "all the appearances of a miniature civil war". Led by Mr. Marchand himself, it began over a contract dispute. Legally, the union should have gone to a government-appointed arbitration board first, but such boards had the reputation of delaying matters indefinitely.

Against the will of the town council, Duplessis sent in a hundred police to occupy the town. Nothing violent occurred, however, until the company tried to bring in strikebreakers. When the strikers planned to resist, they got into a battle with the police and seemed to hold their own rather well until subdued by overwhelming police reinforcements. The police then proceeded to wreak vengeance, reading the Riot Act, raiding, and terrorizing the town in general and the strikers in particular.[1]

As Mr. Marchand indicated, the affair tended to turn people away from Mr. Duplessis and towards the unions.[2] Nevertheless, 1952 saw another similar, serious crisis in a little textile town near Montreal called Louiseville. Once again the police, on the offensive, moved in against the wishes of the town council; once again there was the "reading of the Riot Act, police violence, arbitrary arrests, and other illegal action".[3]

Evidence that Mr. Duplessis could be forced back to some extent by the combined resistance of Quebec's unions is offered by the Murdochville strike of 1957. It involved Gaspé Copper Mines Ltd., and the United Steel Workers of America, an affiliate of the Canadian Labour Congress. All Quebec unions that are not affiliated with Marchand's Confederation are affiliated with the CLC, so that when the Confederation sided strongly with the strikers they had the province's entire labour movement behind them.

After the strike had dragged on for a few months, scores of unionists from all over the province moved into the town, and a great battle took place between them and the company's strikebreakers. The battle was finally stopped by the provincial police; it is notable that while the police were accused of failing to prevent attacks on unionists, they apparently no longer felt free simply to join the company and its strikebreakers in hearty attempts to beat the strikers' brains out, and starve them into submission. Shortly before the strike ended, Mr. Duplessis himself intervened to try to settle things peacefully.[4]

As mentioned in the previous section, Marchand was also leader of the CBC strike of 1959. Commenting on the strike, Marchand thought that the Federal government opposed recognition of the producer's union with no grounds; that the strike became nationalist probably under René Lévesque's influence; that the strike itself is one of the main sources of Mr. Lévesque's nationalism; that the English section of the CBC didn't understand the strikers who had good reason to feel they were being discriminated against.

Marchand looks upon the Minister of Natural Resources, René Lévesque, as a good friend, "perhaps because we went to jail together!" The union chief too was arrested during the March demonstration.

The Confederation does not, however, support any nationalist movement in Quebec and is, according to its president, anti-racist. It is influenced by its setting and is anxious to obtain justice for French Canadians, but not for them exclusively. Marchand believes that the provincial government represents the whole province, not just French Canadians. He reasons that you have a nationalist government when there is perfect coincidence between a particular ethnic group and the government.

Jean Marchand's comments on the Royal Commission on Biculturalism, because he is a member of it, are naturally of a circumspect nature. He makes no secret, however, of his admiration for Mr. André Laurendeau. In the editor, Marchand sees "great intellectual maturity" and expresses the belief that "if something can be done for Canadian unity, he can do it".

Marchand was insistent that Laurendeau be on the commission. If Laurendeau had not been on the commission, Marchand said he would not have agreed to be part of it either. Asked whether he insisted that Laurendeau be co-chairman, Marchand said that the question never arose, as the former's membership and position were decided at the same time.

As to the work of the commission, in Marchand's view, Canadian unity is first of all a political problem — the commission can just help.

In the winter of 1963, the prospects of Social Credit in Quebec seemed highly uncertain. The attitude of Marchand and the Union that he led was not. "I think we are the ones who fought them the hardest", said Marchand. He recalled that he personally held some seventy meetings to argue against Social Credit between the federal elections of June 18, 1962 and those of April 8, 1963. The whole province watched with keen interest a television debate between Marchand and *créditiste* leader Réal Caouette. In all of this, the Unions' champion maintained and repeated as often as he felt necessary that Social Credit's history and philosophy are basically far-right, and opposed to labour. He believes that labour was largely responsible for Social Credit's decline in 1963.

The Unions strongly supported Bill 60, the education bill which is dealt with below in chapter six in the section "Organized Confusion". The workers, according to the president, are especially interested in technical and vocational training. Marchand believes there should be a neutral sector in the public schools for non-Protestants and non-Catholics, and that under Bill 60 neutral schools would be possible. Without Bill 60, a program must be approved by either the Protestant or Catholic Committee. With Bill 60 a Minister could give such approval on his own initiative. Nevertheless, Marchand considers the Bill to be merely one of "transition" — in other words, a compromise.

The labour chief feels that the workers are happier than they were since things began to change, but that the government's policy on labour is still too "broad and general".

SEPTEMBER 13 AND MR. PELLETIER

When the battle's lost and won,
The hurlyburly's but begun.

On September 13, 1759, an army led by the British General Wolfe defeated a French army under General Montcalm on the Plains of Abraham at Quebec City. On September 13, 1959, there was, in the French-Canadian spirit of Quebec, a growing determination to be beaten no more, for the feeling was widespread that during the last two hundred years French Canada had been constantly subjected to perfidious Anglo-Saxon imperialism, and that it had survived by virtue only of its own steadfastness and tenacity. Now it was fed up. "If, after two hundred years, the English still wish to encroach upon us, restrict us, push us around, and meddle in our affairs," said French-Canadian Quebec in effect, "then let them watch out for us! We have not spent these last two hundred years with our hands folded. Now we are strong!"

It is hardly pure coincidence that the second centenary of the Battle of the Plains of Abraham is also the first year of the Quebec revolution.

A misunderstanding about how the centenary was to be observed, if indeed it was to be observed at all, illustrates most acutely the whole question of how English and French Canada should and do feel about each other.

"When a newspaper like *La Presse, Le Devoir* or *L'Action Catholique* receives ten letters on a single theme, it is impressed. Twenty such letters make it sure a major issue is involved. If it should ever receive thirty letters of protest about something, it begins to wonder if the police have enough tear gas to control the coming riot.

"*Eh bien!* On this subject the letters were not numbered in tens, or twenties, or thirties or even hundreds! They got thousands of them!"

Thus did Mr. Gabriel Pelletier, thirty-seven year-old Quebec City lawyer, recently recall the public reaction to an initiative undertaken by the Quebec region of the St. John the Baptist Society (the national association of French Canada) in the spring of 1959. At the time the letters began to come in, around the beginning of June, the president of the region and chief target of it all was Mr. Pelletier himself.

An adequate idea of the seething passions that inspired these missives, as well as of their content, can be drawn from one which appears in *Le Devoir* of June 8, under the title "*Race de Vaincus*" or "Vanquished Race":

"It appears that great rejoicings are in preparation at Quebec. As one must expect, the Fields of Battle will be copiously decorated with red ensigns, and the gaiety of our brave Quebecers will be generously enlivened with the music of 'Rule Britannia' and 'God Save the Queen'. And the occasion that calls for such celebrations, if you please? None other than the second centenary of the Battle of the Plains of Abraham. Never have I read a news item that so greatly grieved me.

"One could read, on the front page of your paper of Thursday, May 28, a press communiqué informing us that on Sunday, the thirteenth of September next, the anniversary of that sadly glorious battle, the national associations, *French* and *English*, of

Quebec will fraternize warmly on the Plains to mark (read carefully) 'the battle which led to the end of the French régime and saw Canada pass into the hands of England'. Just as if there were, for us French Canadians, something to celebrate over. France is beaten. Long live England."

What particularly outrages our unfortunate *Vaincu* is that plans for the celebration were initiated not by St. Andrew's or St. George's or any other English society, but by *La Société St-Jean-Baptiste* itself. He quotes *Le Devoir* as saying that "the president of the St. John the Baptist Society has announced that the celebrations will have, as their theme, 'Two Centuries of Progressive Cooperation.'"
The following is particularly heartrending:

"Mr. Director, there is cause for despair. When the so-called national elite cannot see the odious and absurd nature of a commemoration which associates on the same level, conquerors and conquered, not to say butchers and sacrifices, then that people deserves to be called a vanquished race. To strive, after two hundred years, to stifle in one's breast the bitterness of a military defeat, there is what is Christian; but to invite one's compatriots to climb over the coffins of their glorious dead, the better to kiss the boots of the conqueror, is something against nature."

Despite all the other such letters he read at the time, Mr. Pelletier still remembered this one when it was brought to his attention recently. It is signed Marcel Chaput, Hull.
The reader who has been led into thinking that Mr. Chaput hates the English might consider two other statements by the same person which appear two years later in his book *Pourquoi je suis séparatiste (Why I am a Separatist).*[5]
"This reason (the reason for independence) has nothing to do with the 'damned English' whom, in the first place, I like, and whom I have associated with for twenty years."[6]
With respect to his separatist arguments he writes:

"These are not the words, either, of Anglophobia, born of a sentiment of vengeance that would go back two centuries. If that were the reason for independence, the success of our cause would be seriously compromised, for life teaches us that nothing stable can be built on the burning sands of hatred".[7]

The writer of the letter was Marcel Chaput, Hull. The writer of the book was Dr. Marcel Chaput, Vice-President of *Le Rassemble-*

ment pour l'indépendance nationale (The National Independence Rally).

Most of the letters to the newspapers, including one by another separatist leader, André d'Allemagne, reveal the same point of view as Mr. Chaput's. There are some exceptions. Mr. Pelletier comes to his own defense, and that of his society, in a letter entitled "From Hatred to Love", which appears in the June 12, *Devoir.* "Some people want to treat us as traitors", he begins. "If it is treachery to love, and through love to promise a better lot to one's people, then we have to plead guilty."

Mr. Pelletier goes on to refer to St. Thomas Aquinas, and to the broad principles of Christian charity, temperance, realism, and good-will. "We should love them," he says of the English Canadians. His letter concludes with the following words:

"We desire that 1959 prove, in the face of all fanaticism, that there is place in Canada for a little peace, because there is here a little good will".

In his letter featured in the July 7, *Le Devoir,* entitled "Neither Conquerors nor Vanquished" a Mr. Denis Collerette expresses the view that the French Canadians are not a conquered people but one that has known remarkable progress in the last two hundred years. He disdains those who "under pretext of a false patriotism, tearful with indignation and without maturity, write to you and dare shamelessly to affirm that we are an honourable and illustrious vanquished people." (Here Mr. Collerette is quoting a recent letter).

Editorially, *Le Devoir* tries to look at 1759 dispassionately. In his June 20 editorial Mr. Filion weighs matters in the balance and finds "ridiculous" both those who want to celebrate the anniversary and those who want to mourn it, though the latter only slightly so.

Nevertheless, in August, Mr. Pelletier is forced to resign as president of the St. John the Baptist Society.

Looking back now, that is in 1963, as this chapter is written, to the summer of 1959, Mr. Pelletier ascribes part of his troubles to bad publicity. "We wanted to celebrate not the battle but the collaboration between the French and the English peoples of this province since it took place." He explains: "We wanted to hold these friendly relations up as an example to the rest of the country. But despite our protests, the radio, television and newspapers made out that we were going to celebrate the Battle itself."

Mr. Duplessis, the ex-president feels, may have been behind

the unfavourable reports. Certainly the Premier refused to have the province contribute to the proposed celebration. It is possible, as the following true story will show, that he wished to settle accounts.

It will be remembered that once upon a time a certain Mr. Roncarelli, restaurant owner, displeased Mr. Duplessis by bailing out Jehovah's Witnesses who had been put behind bars by the Provincial Police ("la P.P."). Mr. Duplessis accordingly imposed upon the offender that most crippling of all financial sanctions: he revoked Mr. Roncarelli's license to sell liquor. This was in December, 1946. Mr. Roncarelli at first tried to sue the province, but for this he needed the permission of the Attorney-General, none other than the unyielding Mr. Duplessis. Undaunted, Mr. Roncarelli then pitted himself against the dread Chief in litigious combat before the Supreme Court of Canada. And thus it came to pass that, in January of 1959, or only a little over twelve years after he had lost his license, our heroic David emerged victorious, and Mr. Duplessis was ordered to pay him $33,123.23 in damages.

Now the question was, where could the poor Premier raise the cash?

Shortly after the Supreme Court judgment, the St. John the Baptist Society's section of Boischâtel, which happened to be headed by a good personal friend of the Premier's, decided that it was its patriotic duty to take up a collection for Mr. Duplessis, and set about it right away with commendable efficiency and despatch. Shortly thereafter, a news release from the Premier's office implied that the entire Society was about to rush to the aid of the Leader. Thus Mr. Duplessis' expectations.

They were soon to be rudely disappointed. Through a press communiqué, Mr. Pelletier and his Council let it be known that they deplored the action of Boischâtel and were suspending the section. The communiqué went on to state that Mr. Duplessis, in suspending Mr. Roncarelli's license, had abused his power, and that decisions by Canada's highest court must be respected.

Mr. Duplessis had the reputation of always retaliating against anyone who opposed him. Nevertheless, Mr. Pelletier does not lay all, or even most, of his problems like a wreath of dandelions at the tomb of the late *"dictateur"*. His attempts to establish a good understanding between French and English Canada met with formidable and spontaneous opposition that was attributable only to the French population of Quebec.

For June 24, St. John the Baptist Day, when French Canadians celebrate their national holiday, Mr. Pelletier had a float, depicting a scene from the 1759 Battle, which he wished to enter in the parade. Vehement denunciation, and even threats, hailed the advent of this project. The reaction was quite unrehearsed and had nothing to do with the newspapers. Not to be browbeaten, however, Mr. Pelletier gave final orders to enter the float come what might, even though no sponsor could be found for it. Fortunately, it caused no incidents.

On the same day, accompanied by other notables like Mr. Yvon Tassé, then federal member for Quebec, and Mr. Armand Maltais, the provincial *député*, together with the Consul-General from France and a representative of the British High Commissioner, Mr. Pelletier presented himself at the Wolfe monument (the same one that was to be toppled and smashed in 1963). "I said", he declared now, something like this: "We are not come as a vanquished people, but as a young nation, proud to join its destiny to another people, that together we may build a great new country."

The party then went to the Montcalm monument, where it was received by Lieutenant-Colonel J. Gordon Ross and Mr. Price, representing the city's English associations, who laid wreaths. Mr. Pelletier had at first planned to lay a wreath at the Wolfe monument but had received too many phone calls, threats, and objections even for him.

How does this one-time apostle of peace in Canada and goodwill between two nations feel about it all now, four revolutionary years later?

"You don't get the public up in arms against you the way I did," he recently said, "without doing some very hard thinking about it. I went back to the history books and re-examined every idea I had about the English and French peoples in this country.

"I found that, after all, most of the endeavours towards better cooperation came from our side. You know, at the time of the Conquest, we were already a nation. We were not French, we were Canadians, and called ourselves Canadians — you know the song 'Vive La Canadienne'.

"When the English came, we tried to settle our affairs with them and go on being what we were, Canadians. It was only their attempts to absorb us that made us adopt the adjective 'French' — to call ourselves French Canadians, the better to guard our separate identity.

"Now Confederation is undergoing a crisis that may destroy it. To tell you the truth, I don't know whether it's worth saving or not."

On September 13, 1959, there were no celebrations on the Plains of Abraham. There was a commemoration, properly solemn, at the combined monument to Wolfe and Montcalm beside the boardwalk of Quebec City's Chateau Frontenac. "Simple but touching," the *Quebec Chronicle-Telegraph* described it the next day in a very brief write-up, with a very modest photograph, on page three. Many wreaths were laid. Many grave, important people were present. The immediate past president of the St. John the Baptist Society was present.

THE REVOLUTION

Near the end of his life, Mr. Duplessis' adversaries were forcing him to take the defensive; in a year or two they might have overcome him even had he lived. Nevertheless, until his death on September 7, it is doubtful whether the forces of change in Quebec had quite attained that degree of pressure, of urgency, that one may describe as revolutionary. Before September 7, the veteran warrior, victor of so many political battles, was still dominant, still resisting change. The revolution may have been coming, but few could feel it.

In the fall of 1959, the province — or State — found itself gripped by its first sharp seizure of the new separatism. *Le Devoir* of October 26 features a long letter by Mr. Denis Collerette, trying to combat the growing obsession. When compared, this letter and Mr. Collerette's of July 7, previously discussed, serve to illustrate how quickly our scenes shift. In July it was a question of whether or not English- and French-speaking people could observe a major historical event together. By October, such questions were already irrelevant, dated, *passé*. Now the true issue was whether or not the two peoples could live together in the same country.

The mounting turbulence affected not only English Canada and Confederation, but the purely French Canadian, internal institutions of the State as well. One of the first of these to feel their pressure was, predictably, the educational system. For some time the schools had been undergoing any amount of inquiry, controversy and royal commissioning in the other provinces. In Quebec, on the other hand, very little discussion on the matter could really get under way before a determined attempt was made to establish that, in the first place, hardly anyone spoke French properly.

The full impact of *Le Frère Untel (Brother Anonymous)** is not to be felt until 1960. In observance of our principle of recounting the events of only one year at a time, we shall reserve a full discussion of him for the next chapter. At present it is sufficient to record that his henceforth famous assault on the *"parler joual"*, the (in his eyes) obscene desecration of the French language so coolly perpetrated by French-Canadian school children, and for which he condemns his society, first saw the light of day on November 3, 1959, in the letter columns of *Le Devoir*. It is one of the best proofs one could offer that, at this time, the revolution has indeed begun.

"The State of Quebec Should Act Alone" reads the headline of *Le Devoir*'s major editorial for December 17. The writer, André Laurendeau, is annoyed because Diefenbaker's proposition regarding federal aid to the universities would, he feels, infringe provincial autonomy. Mr. Laurendeau feels that Quebec should follow Mr. Duplessis' example by imposing its own taxes for the money it needs.

No revolution is taking place at Parliament Hill. In the eyes of many leading French Canadians the Federal Government is the same as ever: blind because it will not see Quebec, deaf and dumb because its principal ministers can neither understand nor speak Quebec's language adequately, a model of stolid stupidity and deadness because it shows no feeling even if Quebec all but jabs the honourable members with a spear.

*Literally: Brother so-and-so.

CHAPTER THREE
1960

PAUL SAUVÉ

It is a measure of the true strength then enjoyed by the Union Nationale that the death of Mr. Duplessis did not leave it without high-quality leadership. The picture of health and vitality, brimming with enthusiasm, vigour, and the brave plans inspired by his new role, Mr. Sauvé took over and pressed forward. He had just advanced into 1960 when death cut him down. He had been fifty-two, handsome, forward-looking, the very model of the modern executive, still slim and supple as he attained the pinnacle of success.

Even his political enemies had found little to tax him with beyond the fact that, for so many years, he had been a solid pillar of strength for the Union Nationale.

As we have seen, Mr. Laurendeau attributes the beginning of the psychological revolution to Paul Sauvé. There may be much truth in this idea. Yet what if Mr. Sauvé had lived, and what if he had led his party to yet another electoral success? Might not this have given the province a sense of continuity with former times, and therefore of stability? Might not revolution have given way to orderly evolution under Mr. Sauvé?

True revolution has within it a demonic streak that sets it against all established authority. With Mr. Sauvé's death it seemed that nothing was to be depended upon as the formerly unshakeable representative of authority, the Union Nationale party of Quebec, was severely stricken for the second time in less than four months. It may well be that the rise of the revolution was thus hastened.

WHEN FAIR IS FOUL

The reader will recall that in the spring of 1959, *Le Devoir* carried three front-page articles about Manitoba by Pierre Laporte, and that in all of them Mr. Laporte seemed very well satisfied indeed with the way the province was treating its French-Canadian minority. When, therefore, in a *Devoir* editorial of March 12, 1960,

Mr. Pierre Vigeant describes the school situation in Manitoba as "grave", we may be caught unawares, and perhaps those of us who are not well-versed in the current affairs of the province may, as our first reaction, wonder what dastardly deed of Francophobia its legislature could have perpetrated since the sunny days of 1959. As we read on in the editorial, however, we find more cause for surprise: it turns out that not only has Manitoba done nothing anti-French in the past ten months, but that *Mr. Vigeant is actually reporting on a proposal by the province's royal commission on education that is favourable to the separate schools and to French Canadians in particular. His only concern is that its recommendation in this respect may not be implemented.*

Objectively, the situation of French Canadians in Manitoba tends to improve. In *Le Devoir*, it changes from "nearly one hundred percent" to "grave". Clearly then, *Le Devoir's* view has darkened independently of the news available to it. Four explanations for this fact will be considered here: (1) As we have seen, Alberta's royal commission on education recommended a reduction in the amount of time allowable for French when it reported in 1959. Mr. Vigeant begins his editorial by referring to the situation in Alberta, and since the French Canadian of Quebec generally fails to make any meaningful distinction between one Prairie province and another, he feels that if things are getting worse in one of them, they must be in the others as well. (2) Mr. Vigeant is much more demanding than is Mr. Laporte; Manitoba may seem fine to the latter but he doesn't have his colleague's highly critical disposition. (3) The newspaper has decided to be much more exacting where French-Canadian minorities are concerned. (4) The all-or-nothing spirit of the revolution, a spirit that demands one hundred and not ninety-nine percent, and that cannot tolerate the *near*-observance of French-Canadian rights, now pervades the entire French-speaking population of Quebec — including, of course, that part of it which writes for *Le Devoir*.

The first explanation is almost certainly true and accounts for much of the tone of the Vigeant editorial. The second seems worthless; the author, at least, has no evidence whatever to support it. On the contrary, Mr. Vigeant, it will be remembered, is the man whose only concern with respect to French-Canadian rights seemed to be bilingual cheques, back in 1958. While only the paper's editors know with certainty the value of the third, again the author has no evidence to support the idea that *Le Devoir* has consciously decided to accept nothing less than perfection from English Canada from this point on. That it is infinitely more demanding of English Canada than it had been a year before there can be little doubt, but our fourth explanation accounts admirably for this fact. The revolution can and does make people's outlook change radically without any deliberate decision on their part, for its greatest effects, FLQ bombs notwithstanding, are realized quietly, almost imperceptibly, like those of a colourless, odourless gas. Carbon monoxide from the exhaust of a car can kill its occupants before they can think of leaving it or even turning off the motor; before they realize that anything at all is amiss.

THE TRUE FACE

Characteristic of the past few years in Quebec have been a number of short, often sprightly books about the political preoccupations of the time. Conversational, familiar, written as a rule in the first person, they have tended to bring the revolution home to many who, not at first affected by it themselves, began to wonder what was happening as they felt its winds of change. "Politics Made Easy" could have been the sub-title for all these little volumes.

Nearly all of them were published by *Les Editions de l'Homme* or *Les Editions du Jour.** Appearing on drugstore newstands everywhere, they have given people a sense of being up-to-date in the new Quebec. They have, very often, also helped to propagate the revolution.

Filled with light-hearted sketches, anecdotes and comments about its subject, *Le vrai visage de Duplessis (The True Face of Duplessis)* by Pierre Laporte[1], then the *Devoir* reporter and editorialist whom we have seen in action, now Minister of Municipal Affairs in the Lesage cabinet, is a more or less orderly collection of reminiscences about the mighty man whose career and person the author had followed from day to day as part of his job. It is typical of the politics-made-easy books in most respects, although since revolution is a serious business, the seeming lack of any major axes to grind in this postscript is one important difference between it and most of the series that is to follow.

"Few North American politicians have been the subject of as

---

* A number of them were published in English translation, with critical introductions for the benefit of English readers, by Harvest House of Montreal. These translations and others are referred to in the text and footnotes below.

many cartoons as was Maurice Duplessis," writes Mr. Laporte as he begins his book. . . . "Cartoonists had a choice subject when Duplessis moved or spoke. Moreover, his head lent itself splendidly to caricature. A slightly exaggerated nose and a few pronounced lines were enough to visualize him." [2]

While Mr. Laporte, in his turn, cannot resist the temptation to caricature his subject verbally, his book is perhaps none the worse for it.

"There are three kinds of ministers in the provincial government. Those who can say 'Yes, Maurice', those who say 'Yes, Chief', and . . . Paul Sauvé". [3] Thus, in beginning his chapter "With His Cabinet", does Pierre Laporte quote a Quebec senator to sum up the late Premier's style of leadership. It is also summed up in the famous *Toé, tais-toé* (with "toé" for "toi" this is a slangy "you! keep quiet!"), for sometime thereafter a byword in the province, with which he silenced a minister who wished further to inflate a diatribe that the *Chef* was in the process of delivering for the benefit of a *Devoir* reporter and his (the reporter's) write-ups, of the natural gas commotion. [4]

Toé, tais-toé — the character of a man in three words! Treating his ministers like children, and even like puppets; scolding, praising, rewarding good conduct with prizes and rapping the knuckles of the naughty — himself always busy cracking jokes, putting on a terrific show for the electorate, Mr. Duplessis emerges in *The True Face* as a kind of political *Bonhomme Carnaval* and *"bon papa"* [5] to a whole province.

Everything was under control. What about public opinion? he was once asked. Mr. Laporte quotes him: " 'Do you wish to know what public opinion is? It is the opinion of those who are against us.' " [6] And how many dozens of times did Mr. Duplessis repeat his "Help yourself and heaven will help you. Or help yourself and the Union Nationale will help you. Which comes out the same in the end!" [7] But who would help after Mr. Duplessis? why, Paul Sauvé, of course, for nearly four months.

English Canadians fell easily into the error of thinking of Mr. Duplessis as some kind of Trujillo or other Latin American dictator, enthralling a cowering, helpless people through sheer force of tyranny. True, Duplessis applied various kinds of coercion; true, Duplessis clung to office by every means at his disposal; but true, too, that Duplessis was probably the most admired, perhaps even the most liked man in his province.

He was admired because he was eminently practical, *débrouillard*, adept in the art of always coming out at or near the top, whatever the difficulties to be faced. In the bottom of his heart, every French Canadian, and every English Canadian too for that matter, cherishes the pioneering ideal, the man who, with nothing but an axe, decided that *he* was going to build *his* cabin then and there, Indians or no. With his down-to-earth, rough-and-ready ways, Maurice Duplessis conformed beautifully to this image. He had his feet on the ground, as he loved to repeat.[8] He was the hard-working, sleeves-up, thorough-going professional who has nothing but pity for the fancy intellectuals, the "poets"[9] as he called them.

The following, quoted from chapter five, shows that Duplessis knew when to let up, when not to push too hard. Mr. Laporte quotes a Member: "Sometimes we got fed up with his scenes of anger, his cruel jokes, his dictatorial ways. Was it intuition on his part? He had a gift for redeeming himself by making a great speech, doing something agreeable, turning on his personal charm, and we were won over to him. What had left us disgruntled the day before then seemed like childishness."[10]

And in chapter six, Mr. Laporte describes Mr. Duplessis' techniques in cabinet-management in a way that strongly suggests that, at least among this key group, he was well-liked:

"... When somebody presented him with a gift, a Minister generally ended up receiving it. Duplessis treated his Ministers and Members as a father treats his children. He never forgot to send flowers to a colleague's wife who was in hospital. He was interested in the schooling of the children, in their health. He knew them all by their first names. He even helped to reconcile marriages that seemed on the rocks."[11]

Who would be without such a man?

As for Mr. Duplessis' French, Mr. Laporte describes it thus: "He started sentences and then left them dangling in mid-air without finishing them. He repeated the same things over and over again. His vocabulary was amazingly restricted. He massacred grammar."[12]

Mr. Duplessis said what he pleased as he pleased. *"Toé, tais-toé"* ordered Maurice, and the person thus addressed, though his French were the envy of Paris, knew it was time to hold his tongue.

But after Mr. Duplessis came *Frère Untel,* and the revolution, and all at once correct pronunciation became almost a matter of life or death.

As a man whose fractured French seemed not to worry him in the least, Maurice Duplessis seems scarcely credible now. His Quebec died with him. We may not see his like again.

WHOM ARE THEY AFRAID OF?

If the middle of March, with Mr. Laporte's book, allows us to put aside thoughts of the revolution for a time as we recall other days and other ways, *Le Devoir* soon brings us directly back to the social ferment of 1960.

After *Frère Untel*'s letter of November 3, 1959, on the *"parler joual"*,* *Le Devoir* received, according to Mr. Laurendeau, numerous other letters from lay and religious teachers, likewise protesting against conditions in Quebec's schools, which the writers were seemingly helpless to correct. Indeed, affirms Mr. Laurendeau in his April 8 editorial entitled "Whom Are They Afraid Of", the teachers, regardless of how mature and reasonable their arguments may be, apparently live in fear and trembling lest anyone discover that they are thinking; they sign all their letters with pen names and fervent supplications to merciful Mr. Laurendeau, that he whisper no word of their true identities. "Could there," Mr. Laurendeau wonders, almost innocently, "could there be, then, a certain form of persecution, a certain menace to liberty?"

Frère Untel (as we later learn in his apocalyptic book) hesitates. He suffers "real anguish". He consults an eminent priest.[13] Finally he acts, and in *Le Devoir* of April 30, a whole twenty-two days after Mr. Laurendeau's thoughtful questions, comes his all-demolishing *réponse*. Victims of a sick love of safety and security, buried alive in the traditions of the past, the schools, charges *Frère Untel*, and by extension the French-Canadian society that builds, nourishes, and mans them, are afraid to say or do anything on their own.

Thus our humble Brother, himself letting fall the cloak of fear with a single twist of his powerful young shoulders, stands revealed, the era's first true revolutionary. Five months later, he will be the talk of the province.

THE CHRISTIAN AND THE ELECTIONS

"A Sensational Book by the Abbés Dion and O'Neill: *Le chrétien et les élections (The Christian and the Elections)* 'We Must Translate the Thought of Our Bishops into Daily Practice' ".

° On speaking a corrupt French (Ed.).

It is in these terms that the major *Devoir* headline of May 4, 1960, seven weeks before the provincial election of that year, hails the advent of the book[14] we are now to consider, complete with photographs of the authors and Canon Racicot, who has written the preface. Sources for the book include pontifical and episcopal texts, historical documents, and diverse commentaries about political morality. All of these tend to give it a very careful, moderate, measured tone; it is not highly-placed representatives of the Church, after all, who feel called upon to make rousing appeals to public passions.

What is audacious is getting all this material together and blazoning it like a red flag before the electorate at this time. Just how extraordinary such an action is can be gathered from the words of a female parishioner as quoted by Canon Racicot in his preface:

"You always preach about mysteries, about parts of the *Credo*, about grace and the sacraments, about the commandments of God and the Church, about sanctification of Sunday, about blasphemy, about all the forms of concupiscence, and, in particular about sexual problems, and upon my word you preach remarkably well! But you hardly ever preach about the civic virtues; in particular, about the different forms of social justice, about honesty in contracts, respect for one's word, the rights and duties of a good citizen, and the profound transformations that modern life brings to the behaviour of humans."[15]

Seven weeks before the election! A good time to make up for past failings!

The most striking part of the book is the appendix. While all the preceding chapters deal with problems of political morality in a general, abstract, theoretical way, the appendix hits hard at (what was then) the here and now of alleged political venality in the Province of Quebec.

"Political Immorality in the Province of Quebec", as the chapter that forms the appendix is titled, turns out to be the reprint of an article that the abbés Dion and O'Neill had originally published in 1956, in denunciation of what they felt to be flagrant abuses of the provincial election then just past. Avant-garde, radical, a little before their time in 1956, the abbés come into their own four years later as the revolution gathers momentum.

Statements like "The exhibition of stupidity and immorality that Quebec has just witnessed cannot leave any thinking Catholic indifferent. . . . It is pitiful that this people (the people of Quebec) reconciles with such extraordinary facility such manifest and generally accepted venality with a religiosity no less manifest and accepted ... An electoral period such as that which we have just been through must be declared an instrument of demoralization and anti-Christ,"[16] set the tone of the article.

In normal times complacently set aside as exaggerated, such criticism can only be accepted when a revolution is either about to begin or already in progress. For a people cannot endorse opinions as sulphurous as these unless it is ready to despair of itself, to do or die, to try anything in the sure conviction that matters cannot possibly deteriorate any further.

It Has to Change

Il faut que ça change − *It has to change* − is the slogan chosen by the provincial Liberals for 1960. While they evidently mean it to apply above all to the governing party, one cannot but admire how neatly it sums up the spirit of the times in a general way. What must change? Why, nearly everything, if the new Quebec is not to be still-born!

Foremost among the apostles of change are *Le Devoir*, with *Frère Untel* and his sympathizers in its letter columns; the abbés Dion and O'Neill, the separatists and semi-separatists; fortune herself, since the Union Nationale's two top men have just disappeared, and even those who, without knowing quite why, just think that the government has been there long enough.

The Liberals win but narrowly, nonetheless. Their opponents are not to be crushed easily. Moreover, potent as it is, even the revolution takes time and is at this point only ten months old.

Brother Anonymous

More than any other manifestation of the new era, more than *Le Devoir* or René Lévesque, more than the nationalization of electric power, Marcel Chaput, the wondrous, strange architecture of some of the recently-built churches − more even than FLQ bombs − *The Impertinences of Brother Anonymous (Les insolences du Frère Untel)*, first published on August 30, 1960,* prefaced by and dedicated to André Laurendeau and to a certain Michel Golaneck, humble Ukrainian of virtuous obscurity, *is* the revolution. Extravagant actions and projects, vaunted cure-alls,

---

* Published by Les Editions de L'Homme in 1960 and, in translation, by Harvest House of Montreal in 1962.

promised political miracles — all these proceed from the revolution: *Les insolences* is the pure essence of it all, distilled and put into words. In the months following its appearance, it sets sales records that no other Canadian book has been able to touch in a single year.

"I work with the axe, though I don't like to," Brother Anonymous warns us. "By temperament I am rather delicate, and nostalgic about the past. I enjoy Oka cheese and coffee laced with brandy. But in the land of Quebec this is no time for delicacy. When everybody talks *joual*, it's no time to watch the fine points of grammar. If a man is asleep in a house on fire, the neighbours don't wake him up with Mozart's *Eine Kleine Nachtmusik*. They yell at him, and if he still sleeps soundly, they kick him out of bed."[17]

In the fiery view of Brother Anonymous, the abbés Dion and O'Neill are so staidly prudent that he is at a loss to understand how people could ever have been agitated by them:

"Why do the writings of the two abbés, their principal books, cause so much commotion? Read and reread these texts, and you will find nothing to justify the hysteria of the beadles. Far from being extravagant, their works are perfectly moderate, prudent and calm. Indeed they are far more calm, more polite than the texts of the virtuous inquisitors who denounce them."[18]

When a revolution is on, what is daring today may be unenterprising, hardly worth mentioning, the day after tomorrow. One year after the Quebec revolution begins to move, and three months after they make headlines, our abbés find themselves — perhaps not quite *passé,* but "moderate, prudent, calm".

As the theme quotation for his first chapter, Brother Anonymous chooses the following quotation from Léon Bloy: "We are proud of being vanquished, we play and work as vanquished men. We laugh, we weep, we love, we write, we sing as the vanquished. All our moral and intellectual life can be explained by this single fact, that we are cowardly dishonoured vanquished men."[19]

Brother Anonymous does not mention that Léon Bloy is a French literary figure who lived from 1846 to 1917, ultra-aggressive and caustic, but having no discernible connection with Canada or Quebec. But what's the difference: a bomb explodes just as well whether it comes from France or Belgium or Moscow.

The first chapter (Part One), titled "The Language of Defeat", is an attack on the *"parler joual"*. It will be recalled that *Frère Untel* (or *Frère Untel* as he originally was) first came to public attention on November 3, 1959, with a letter dedicated to the same subject. Chapter one may give us a sense of having been there before, since in part it reproduces the letter word for word; but it is, taken as a whole, a bold and dashing enlargement on the original composition.

What is *"joual"*?

"The word joual is a summary description of what it is like to talk *joual*, to say *joual* instead of *cheval, horse*. It is to talk as horses would talk if they had not long since plumped for the silence and the smile of Fernandel . . . . I can't write joual down phonetically. It can't be fixed in writing for it is a decomposition, and only Edgar Poe could fix a decomposition. You know the story where he tells of the hypnotist who succeeded in freezing the decomposition of a corpse — It's a wonderful horror story."[20]

As he regards the present state of affairs in the society round about him, the revolutionary is filled with loathing, disgust, horror.

Untel's pupils, far from being concerned about their speech, seem quite proud of it, which fact gives rise to the following comment:

"Of course joual-speakers understand each other. But do you want to live your life among joual speakers? As long as you want merely to chat about sports and the weather, as long as you talk only such crap, joual does very well. For primitives, a primitive language is good enough; animals get along, with a few grunts. But it you want to attain to human speech, joual is not sufficient."[21]

The terrible English, of course, are responsible for a lot. Besides the quotation from Léon Bloy, we have also the following:

"What can we do? The whole French Canadian society is foundering. Our merchants show off their English company names, the bill-boards along our roads are all in English. We are a servile race; our loins were broken two hundred years ago, and it shows.[22]

If the government arranges evening courses, "The most popular are the English classes. . . . Accounting is taught in English, with English textbooks, in the Catholic Province of Quebec, where the system of teaching is the best in the world."[23]

Chapter two, "Education for Heaven", sets to the basic work of revolution, that is tearing down the established authority, with a vengeance. His big axe slicing flesh, Brother Anonymous applies himself to the respectable task of cutting up the authority which, outside of the Church, has the most direct control over him, the Department of Public Instruction.

The principal affirmations and charges of the chapter may be summed up as follows: the Department was set up not for any positive purpose but to avoid the perils of Protestantism and Anglicization; everything in the secondary course — programs, books, teachers — is improvised; one can never get a clear statement from the Department or find anyone in it who accepts responsibility; the courses are poorly planned and the teachers know nothing.

After having charged the Department with incompetence, irresponsibility, and with obstructing where it should guide, Brother Anonymous suggests that it be mercifully disposed of:

"I am soft-hearted, you know. I wouldn't hurt anybody. Still, we must close down the Department. Let's give all the officials all the medals there are, not forgetting the one for Agricultural Merit. Let's create some special ones, such as one for Solemn Mediocrity. Let's give them all a comfortable and well-paid retirement and send them home to their mamas."[24]

Does one imagine that the Brother is joking, that he will not be backed by public opinion? On November 15, 1960, Mr. Jean Lesage said: "There is no question, and there never will be, under my administration, of creating a minister of public instruction." Yet as this is written, in the fall of 1963, the government has a bill to create just that, with the Department of Youth and of Public Instruction to be fused into the new Ministry of Education. Exit the despised Department of Public Instruction of Brother Anonymous?

Not yet. The conservative forces mobilized for a real fight around the government's famous Bill 60.

In chapter three, we learn that "The failure of our system of teaching is the reflection of a failure or, at any rate a paralysis, of thought itself. . . . What we practise here is purity through sterilization, orthodoxy through silence, security through dull repetition. We imagine there is only one way to go straight, and that is never to set out; one way never to make mistakes and that is never to experiment; one way not to get lost and that is to stay asleep."[25]

Our section "Whom Are They Afraid Of", earlier in this chapter, refers to Brother Anonymous' reply to André Laurendeau's questions about why teachers were afraid to give their names. This reply is reproduced in its entirety in chapter four, "Quebec's

Jansenist Shudders". Complaining of an atmosphere of stifling religious domination, the Brother writes of preaching professors:

"They renounce money. They renounce sex. They never renounce power. Poor and chaste, but domineering, full of arrogance. 'The kings of the nations have lordship over them. But ye shall not be so, but he that is greater among you, let him become as the younger, and he that is chief as he that . . . serve' ".[26] Protesting still further, after enlarging upon his views of how authority should be exercised among Christians, Anonymous boldly asserts that "When the Protestants left the paternal mansion (I might as well borrow John XXIII's metaphor) they carried some good with them, a small part of the heritage. We were left with the old property, the house and the equipment; they got away with a few pennies worth of liberty."[27]

Farther on in the chapter, the state of religion in Quebec is described in the following terms: "Things are already more spoiled than shows on the surface. The pilgrimages to Notre Dame du Cap and Ste. Anne de Beaupré ought not to fool us. In Spain too . . . the places of pilgrimage were very popular right up to 1936. The priests were held in high honour. Until the day they were shot, more than a thousand of them in the diocese of Barcelona alone.

"Spoiled beyond what we can see — the young people whom we teach in class are as far from Christianity as they can go without making a commotion. Their ideas, their feelings, above all their feelings about money, women, success, love are as foreign to Christianity as is possible."[28]

The province thought it all true. "He's only saying out loud what the rest of us have been saying quietly to ourselves", was a comment one might often hear on *Les Insolences*.

Over and above the impression made by his ideas, *Le Frère Untel* doubtless owed much of his popularity to an attractive combination of youth and vitality with bluff good humour, wit, and flamboyant recklessness. Sales might not have been quite so astounding but for passages like the following:

"Good old *Devoir*, brotherly old *Devoir*, cheers! Cheers for good old Filion! They've been saying that you grow old and prudent. No matter, you struck a stout blow for freedom. And cheers for you, Laurendeau, so sensitive and human, and for all the staff of *Le Devoir*. How I would like to meet a bishop of whom I would want to say, Cheers, good old bishop! I don't say there aren't any, but I've never met one."[29]

The anonymous celebrity did not long remain so, but was identified as Brother Pierre-Jérôme,* a teaching Marist serving in St-Joseph d'Alma. Before long he was required to go to Rome, and eventually to Switzerland, to further his theological studies. It seems hardly probable that *La Belle Province* will see him again. At thirty-three his mission was accomplished.

GOODBYE MR. BARRETTE

In mid-September, just over a year after Duplessis' death, a red *Devoir* headline announced the resignation of Mr. Antonio Barrette as leader of the Union Nationale party. He had been chosen leader after the death of Paul Sauvé; before the June elections, Union Nationale advertisements frequently represented him as one of *Les trois grands* of the Union Nationale, the first two being his immediate predecessors. The Liberals, in their turn, had had considerable success with their mockery of his reference to his working-class origins: cartoons of Mr. Barrette always showed him with his *"boîte à lunch"* (lunch pail). Now he was already history as far as the politics of the province were concerned.

Disagreement over the administration of the party was given as the cause for his departure.

THERE SHOULD BE NO CANADIANS

The year 1960 ends with French-Canadian Quebec, still having to fight as always against assimilation, rebelling strenuously against the proposed inclusion of the word "Canadian" among the answers to the question of ethnic origin — a matter that was already, it will be remembered, an issue in the spring of 1959. Now, with time running out, and with an infinitely more aggressive spirit than it had had a year previously in any case, Quebec was ready to resist with all the strength it could muster.

It is doubtful that the separatists really needed any further help from the federal government at this time. Needed or not, it was being generously donated.

* Since the book was written and probably as a result of the criticism contained in it of the florid pseudonyms with which the brothers were saddled inside the order, the rules were changed and Brother Pierre-Jérôme was known by his given and family names of Jean-Paul Desbiens.

CHAPTER FOUR
1961

.

THERE ARE NO CANADIANS

1960 passes into 1961 with no slackening in Quebec's intensifying opposition to the answer "Canadian" in the census, as previously explained. Finally the struggle reaches its peak. On January 19, *Le Devoir*'s banner headline is "Quebec Asks Ottawa to Cross Out the Word 'CANADIAN'".

Victory in Ottawa Day is January 24. "Ottawa Eliminates all Reference to a 'CANADIAN' Origin" reads the red *Devoir* headline.

Officially, there are no Canadians, at least none who can forget about who their ancestors were.

AFTERGLOW

As 1961 begins the revolution is some sixteen months old. Its first full year is complete. Lingering in the minds of Quebecers, its afterglow provokes a reflective mood in the early winter months, a first search for the essential meaning of the new phenomenon. Near the end of January, Les Editions de l'Homme, the book's publishers, announce that, four months after its appearance, the sales of *Les insolences du Frère Untel* have passed the hundred-thousand mark.

Le Magazine Maclean,[1] the French-language counterpart of *Maclean's* makes its début in February. Mr. André Laurendeau, with the first of his columns about Quebec, the University of Montreal professor, Mr. Michel Brunet, with his review of French Canada's awakened nationalism, and Adèle Lauzon with her inevitable write-up, generously supplemented with photographs, on *Le Frère Untel*, all reflect the public's interest in the events of the past months. Now, in 1963, a little over two years later, their opinions and points of view seem to belong to another world.

André Laurendeau's column is headed with the customary small snapshot, the one of him that is so often reproduced, showing him chin in hand, questioning, perhaps a little bored, perhaps a little tired, as though waiting for someone to do something. The title of his article, "Will the Liberal Government Be Only Conservative?" seems to bear out the impression made by the photograph.

Meditative, Mr. Laurendeau retraces the steps taken by Quebec's provincial government from the last days of Duplessis up to his time of writing. The following excerpts from his article illustrate how he regards the Liberal government that *Le Devoir* has so strongly supported. After acknowledging that the Liberals made some improvements when they began, Mr. Laurendeau expresses his reservations:

"Since then, the picture has become rather cloudy, and difficulties are beginning.

"One has sometimes from the outside the impression of a slow-down, at least of some hesitation — which relates to the objectives and not only the means . . . Will the government get old too quickly? Does it have, and does the party have, a living faith in its program? I have no doubts about a Lapalme, a Lesage, a René Lévesque and a few others: will this yeast be enough to raise the dough? . . . The government must accept its responsibilities to govern . . . otherwise it will be . . . a good, conservative, Paul Sauvé government."[2]

Not only is the splendid new Quebec not moving very fast, one might conclude, but it is in imminent danger of stopping altogether. We must, though, remember who is writing about it. To a racing-car driver, seventy-five miles per hour is a slow-down. To Dr. Marcel Chaput, the French Canadians are a people sadly deficient in national pride.

Frère Untel, overflowing with youthful energy, bursts upon the Quebec scene like a supernova, for a few months giving off enormous quantities of heat and light, and then is seen no more.[*] Born in 1912, his "godfather" André Laurendeau, to whom he owes even his new baptism (the pen name *Frère Untel* was invented by the

[*] By September 1963, however, the English translation, *The Impertinences of Brother Anonymous* was in its fourth printing. The reviewer in *The Educational Courier* of Ontario (May-June 1963), probably English Canada's most influential teacher's journal, among other enthusiastic comments had this to say of the book: "Do you know what *joual* is? It is a recently invented word for the corrupt speech of French Canadians. There should be a word for our *joual*, the corrupt speech of English Canadians. . . . In the book, Brother Anonymous discusses solutions, a civilized approach to this all-pervading problem. . . . [Corrupt speech out of a corrupt context] From hilarious cover to gentle farewell, this is a book for teachers to savour. . . . Summer whodunits you can find for yourself . . . but spare a few hours for Brother Anonymous, great teacher, and teacher of teachers" [Ed.].

Editor), exerts his steady force year after year, becoming, very possibly, a little more influential with each passing day.

The Editor-in-chief of *Le Devoir* will not thrust revolution upon you; he is far too discreet, too aware of your sensibilities. He may, however, *suggest* revolutionary changes, quietly, moderately, tactfully, with due regard for alternatives; led on inevitably, or so it would seem, by the sheer logic of things.

Michel Brunet's article is entitled "The Evolution of Nationalism in French Canada, from the Conquest to 1961". Commenting upon the upsurge of nationalism then in progress, he writes:

"How many politicians, journalists, and university people, who displayed, not very long ago, violent anti-nationalist sentiments, today defend the theses and the ideals of French Canadian nationalism?"[3]

The professor then explains that the federal Conservative win of 1957, showed that a party could take power without Quebec's support; the "hardly recommendable" way the English-Canadian Liberals disposed of Mr. St. Laurent as leader, and the crushing Conservative majority of 1958, which could do without Quebec, all made Quebecers feel that they could be effective only within their own province.

"The Province of Quebec, which seemed fixed once and for all in complete political and social immobility, has been transformed since about a year ago into a sort of little volcano, still harmless, it's true, but rather noisy."[4]

This comment of Adèle Lauzon's, in her article about *Frère Untel,* is probably a good short summary of the way many, if not most, Quebecers feel about their province in early 1961.

REPRESSION?

In the two years between June 1959 and June 1961, Dr. Marcel Chaput comes a very long way indeed. Readers will remember his foaming epistle in condemnation of Mr. Pelletier's proposed association among French- and English-speaking people to mark the second centenary of the Battle of the Plains of Abraham. June 1961, finds him not only a leader in a flourishing new separatist organization, but a nationalist hero who appears to have excellent chances of acquiring the crown of a martyr.

A scientist working for the Defense Research Board, Dr. Chaput becomes known for his separatist activities. In consequence, the Board, in effect doing all it can to speed the separatists on their way, asks him to resign.

Is this the beginning of repression? Overnight the name of Marcel Chaput is on all French Canadian lips; the man who had been just another private citizen is, thanks to his superiors, instantly transformed into a major public figure.

Not unresponsive to such flattering attention, Dr. Chaput is soon to explain what Separatism is all about in the book we shall now consider.

Compulsory Childhood

In *The Impertinences,* Brother Anonymous expresses keen dissatisfaction that he and his fellow teaching Brothers are, in his belief, being held in a state of suffocating bondage; that they are being kept down, baffled and frustrated in their legitimate aspirations, treated like moronic children. For this unhappy order of things, he places the blame at the doors of the Department of Public Instruction, people having authority within the Church, and by extension, in French Canada in general.

For Dr. Marcel Chaput, in his book, *Why I Am a Separatist,* the hated authority is English Canada and the Federal Government (for which he was working when he wrote); the basic discontent that he feels, however, seems much like that of the Brother. One of the most striking features of his book is the number of times he speaks of French Canada as being in a state of enforced dependence from which it can only escape by declaring its independence loud and clear, for all to hear. Skimming the pages, we find that the word *"tutelle"* (tutelage) appears time and again. French Canada apparently sits before English Canada like a pupil before his tutor.

The following are some quotations from the book to illustrate this point: "It seems to me that the French Canadians who are free are even rarer than one would have thought — which is normal for a people in tutelage.[5] . . . It (bilingualism) is simply a reflex, conditioned by two hundred years of tutelage.[6] . . . And the French-Canadian nation is a nation . . . that lives in economic tutelage.[7] . . . Economically, the French Canadians are a people in tutelage.[8] . . . It pays to be Anglicized and kept in tutelage.[9] . . . The time has come for French Canada to cut the umbilical cord that chokes it, otherwise it will condemn itself to die of infantilism.[10] . . . Since two hundred years ago, French Canadians have undergone political tutelage, economic tutelage, cultural tutelage, social tutelage, and over and above all tutelages, psychological tutelage."[11]

We have given here just a sampling of Dr. Chaput's references to "tutelage" and immaturity in describing his people.

The nasty English, they're so mean, they just won't let us poor French Canadians grow up, seems to be the message.

Is Dr. Chaput trying to win sympathy from adolescents whose fathers refuse to give them the car as often as they would like it? Does he feel that he is not being allowed to grow up? Does he think that French Canadians in general don't grow up?

The Impertinences of Brother Anonymous does offer one passage on the bad-old-English-won't-let-us-do-what-we-want theme. Seemingly unaware that the revolution is under way despite his leading role in it, the good Brother writes:

"We are among the few western nations who have known neither political revolution nor major political crisis. We shall have no revolution; the proximity of our Anglo-Saxon neighbours guarantees that. They would not let us do any damage. Perhaps even the Twenty-Second Regiment (the Vandoos), commanded in English, would put it down."[12]

Nevertheless, in general, Brother Anonymous does little projecting; he seems to feel that French Canada itself is responsible for most of its ills.

The revolution strives mightily to break all chains. The French Canada of Dr. Chaput finds itself floundering manfully in chains of servitude and inferiority that are historical, political, economic, cultural, social, numerical, and (a separatist never spares his adjectives) perhaps above all psychological.[13] In separatist doctrine, all these chains have been locked to *Canadien* limbs by the terrible Anglo-Saxon ogre; and all are to fall with a resounding crash at a touch of the good fairy's Independence Wand.

Since revolution is a product of desperation, passages of the book that describe matters as being as bad as they possibly can be, so that any alternative whatever appears preferable, are in the main-stream of the larger phenomenon.

The biggest threat to French Canada, at least in nationalist eyes, is the possibility that it will eventually disappear altogether, be assimilated. Unless Quebec obtains independence, Dr. Chaput warns, assimilation will indeed erode away its very existence:

"By assimilation, you probably understand the condition of the former French Canadian who, after living in English territory, has completely lost his language. Perhaps he has never spoken French, being born of parents who were themselves totally Anglicized. You are right. But that is not the only form of Anglicization.

"People do not seem to realize that the assimilation of a people is not a mushroom phenomenon, a surprise event. One day one is French and the next, one is so no longer. In reality, assimilation is a process more gradual than is believed. As with virtue, temperature, or autonomy, there are degrees. In Canada, all French Canadians are more or less assimilated. And this assimilation has nothing to do with the friendship or hostility that one may show towards Anglo-Canadians or Americans.

"The merchant across the street who uses an English name although he is French-speaking, that is assimilation. That other, like thousands in Quebec, who reads only English magazines and newspapers, who looks at or listens almost uniquely to English radio-television, that is assimilation. That youth of ours who knows only the hit parade, that is assimilation. The city hall that hoists the Red Ensign in Quebec on every holiday, that is assimilation. All these tourist establishments that disfigure the French visage of our province, thinking they will draw American visitors, that is assimilation. The French university that believes itself forced to teach with the help of American manuals, that is assimilation.

"Or at least, that is a degree of assimilation, while waiting for the next degree. And so on through the years, until one day, a day like all the others, one has no longer any desire to be what one has been.

"Unhappily, it is not arms that assimilate peoples. It would be too easy to resist. It is interests, currents of thought, modes, psychological climates, in brief, it is the situation like the one in which we find ourselves.

"With a little perseverance, we will attain, no doubt, we too, and perhaps soon, that day like all the others when we will no longer insist on becoming what we have been, that is French Canadians."[14]

In the virtually hopeless situations described by the revolutionary, the temptation to look for a cure-all is practically irresistible. Although, in a realistic mood, he sometimes denies that it will solve all problems, separatism's qualifications as a cure-all are seen by Dr. Chaput in the following light:

"Everything that French Canada is reproached with, its dis-

ordered speech, its lack of boldness, of pride, its inferiority complex, and the rest, is in reality the symptoms that proceed from a
cause. And to wish to change a people by trying to correct these
morbid symptoms is dangerous and illusory therapy. To wish that,
through pure sentiment, French Canadians remain true to French
culture, to their origins and their traditions, is to ask for a heroism
that no people could show for very long. A people does not look
after its culture for that culture. To last, this fidelity that one wants
of it must be supported by its life. A culture that doesn't give a
man his living is a culture destined to disappear. That's why the
French-Canadian problem demands an over-all solution."[15]

Everything — scandals like that of the natural gas, electoral
immorality, slang, inefficiency in education, sanctimonious hypo-
crisy in religion, to name a few of the more prominent vices with
which French Canadians have been charging themselves just before the book appears — everything that French Canada is reproached with can be attributed to the fact that it is not yet a
sovereign, independent state.

Is one concerned about the depredations wrought by that scur-
rilous, blubber-tongued young miscreant called *Joual?* Precocious
"Pupil Chaput" has the answer to that, too:

" 'Pupil Chaput, when do you think that the French Canadians
will cease to talk *joual?*' "

" 'When Quebec has become French, Sir the Inspector.' "

" 'Pupil Chaput, how in your belief can Quebec become French?' "

" 'First, by proclaiming its political sovereignty in order to apply
an over-all solution.' "

" 'Second, by decreeing French, the only official language.

" 'Third, by thus rendering French necessary and profitable.

" 'Fourth, by surveying the correction of all that is printed and
displayed.

" 'Fifth, by rehabilitating in our eyes France and its culture. . .' "[16]

There are ten recommendations in all. Again presenting his magic remedy the separatist writes:

"If our people suffers from Anglomania, if it thinks only of ex-
hibiting itself in English, if it speaks the bad French that it speaks,
it is that the life of a minority has not taught it the respect of its
language, the pride of its origins. How could one be surprised
that there is in the people so little national pride when, since the
Conquest, and especially since 1867, so many of our guides, so

many of our career politicians, so many of our masters of thought have amputated us from our most legitimate aspirations, when in the name of good understanding and national unity, we have been proposed only the compromises that we were always the only ones to pay for?" [17]

Alas, for a people with "so little national pride". Thus the reasoning of Dr. Marcel Chaput, biochemist; Vice-President of the *Rassemblement pour l'indépendance nationale* in September 1961, when *Why I Am a Separatist* appears; President of the movement a month later.

Her Majesty's Loyal Opposition

The revolution cries out urgently that it's now or never, that the old must die and the new be born. "But how?" asks an anxious province. And the separatists come rushing up with their answer, written on great placards, waving over their heads. 1961 is a soul-stirring year for them.

It must not be imagined, however, that their opposition is not formidable. The contrary is so true that even the dead would rise to denounce them.

"*J'ai choisi l'indépendance (I Chose Independence)* constitutes a fascinating debate between Henri Bourassa and Raymond Barbeau, founder-president of the LAURENTIAN ALLIANCE. It's an indispensable document for anyone who wishes to understand the protagonists of a sovereign Quebec."

Thus, in part, reads the cover advertisement for another little book[18] that appears in September.

The cover must evoke no little astonishment. A debate with the illustrious founder of *Le Devoir,* the giant who shook the power of Sir Wilfrid Laurier? But he's been dead since 1952! How can one possibly have a debate with him?

Mr. Barbeau manages it. His basic plan is simple enough. For chapter one he takes a few lines from a speech pronounced by Mr. Bourassa in 1923. Then he overrules and overbears Mr. Bourassa, and, as it were, stamps about on his grave for a while. For chapter two, he takes another few lines from the same speech and repeats his performance. And so on, till the end of the book.

What could Henri Bourassa have said in 1923 so potent that the separatists of 1961 still have to worry about it? Since this is a book about the revolution, we cannot reproduce the whole of Mr.

Bourassa's speech here, but the excerpts chosen for attack by Mr. Barbeau in his first three chapters will perhaps reveal in some measure what the Laurentian is up against:

"Whatever happens, the whole of the Canadian Confederation is no less, for the time being, the country of all Canadians, ours like that of the Anglo-Canadians; it imposes on all the same duties, it commands the same love, not perhaps of heart, but of conscience, honour, and reason. On this point, I insist on being precise.

"Since a short time ago, a group of young French Canadians, brilliant, eloquent, has been doing all it can to be ready, in the expectation of the rupture, for the formation of a French state, the limits of which would approximately correspond to those of the present Quebec. It is, they say, the ideal towards which we should move. Is this dream realizable? I do not think so. Is it desirable? I don't believe that any more, neither from the French point of view nor, even less, from the Catholic point of view, which takes precedence, in my eyes, over the French interest.

"Realizable, it could not be, except by a conjunction of events and circumstances so improbable that it would be idle, unless one had a lot of time and words to waste, to stop and think about them. To attempt that realization, whether in the existing conditions or those more difficult that one can foresee in the future, would bring upon us the animosity, the distrust, and the combined opposition of the whole of English Canada and the United States, to say nothing of England; and that opposition would have as points of support the formidable economic interests concentrated in the city of Montreal, and possessing already a notable portion of our public domain and our natural resources."[19]

Diametric opposition to the separatists is in no sense confined to the past. Typical of 1961 anti-separatism is Mr. Gilles Boyer: in the September 30 edition of *Le Soleil*, Quebec City's major French-language daily, Mr. Boyer takes advantage of the occasion offered by his review of the Chaput and Barbeau books to refute the entire separatist position.

Boyer sees no basis for the separatists' dreams of joy in a rich and rosy independent Quebec. He points out that secession would be unconstitutional and might well be opposed militarily. Even without resorting to arms, the surrounding continent could exert all kinds of pressure against the new state, for the Americans would favour it no more than they do Cuba. Economically, Quebec would be a "small, isolated market of five million consumers", walled in by the high tariffs of its angry and vengeful neighbours. Would it, Mr. Boyer asks, be ready to seek help in the arms of Russia?

The journalist concludes that separatism is a last resort only, premature in a province that is just beginning to exploit the powers and liberties it has under the Constitution.

WE DON'T NEED YOU

"The Canadian Experiment, Success or Failure?" was the subject of the First Congress on Canadian Affairs, which was organized by the General Association of the Students of Laval University and took place from November 15 to 18, 1961. A full account of its proceedings was published by Laval University Press in 1962, and it is this that we use as a reference.[20]

Collaborating in the Congress were the Honourable Jean Lesage, E. Davie Fulton, and René Lévesque, together with Messrs. Murray G. Ballantyne, Jean-Jacques Bertrand, Marcel Chaput, Douglas Fisher, Eugene Forsey, Maurice Lamontagne, André Laurendeau, James R. Mallory, Michael Oliver, Gérard Pelletier, and Mason Wade.

Student representatives were present from nearly all Canadian universities.

One of the chief objects of the Congress appears to have been to induce a better understanding between French- and English-speaking university students first, and the Canadian public in general, secondly, about what Confederation is and should be. While it is impossible to assess the degree to which this purpose was realized, it was perhaps not greatly furthered by the Department of National Defense and the Federal member of parliament for Port Arthur, Mr. Douglas Fisher.

Dr. Marcel Chaput, as one of those invited to speak, asked permission to take leave from his work with the Defense Research Board at Ottawa so that he might attend the Congress. When permission was virtuously refused (the idea!) our repressed chemist, triumphantly independent, announced that he was going anyway. The book on the Congress describes his welcome at Quebec as "tumultuous".[21]

Suspended from his job for two weeks when he returned to Ottawa, he was then able to resign gloriously and devote all his time to L'indépendance. Thus Dr. Chaput and all his federal partners.

After making his speech, the Honourable René Lévesque said that he thought English Canada needed French Canada more than the reverse.[22] Scorched by this ember from Quebec's political fires, Mr. Douglas Fisher made sure that when his turn came he would tell the honourable minister just how much he thought English Canada needed French Canada.

"I am tempted to say," he asserted, in reference to the provocative comment, 'That goes double!' ... If I could come down without too great seriousness upon this whole question of French Canada from an English-Canadian point of view, it might go like this. If I was speaking to my constituents or anybody from Sudbury westward, trying to explain what little I know about French Canadians, their reaction would be: 'Well, what has the French Canadian to offer us, that we should be so excited about *bonne entente* and learning the French language and so on?' And I wonder what they would say about French-Canadian culture? I suppose for us the greatest impact of French-Canadian culture has been made by Maurice Richard and Lili St-Cyr. We did have Gisèle, of course, but she became Gisèle McKenzie and went off to the United States. I wonder whether we are to be fascinated by your marvellous police tradition, the magnificence of your telegraphers, the ingenuity that I witnessed when I was looking into the operation of the Jacques-Cartier bridge in Montreal. I wonder if we are to be so tremendously impressed with the Courtemanches, the Pouliots, the Sévignys and such people whom we encounter at Ottawa. I wonder if we are to be impressed with your tradition of literary censorship, or whether your educational system has a great deal to offer us in a society where technocracy is becoming so much more important. I cannot honestly say I believe that we need your resources. You have lots of iron ore here, but so have we and so has much of the rest of Canada. You have a lot of base metals, but so have we. You have lots of water power, but so has British Columbia; and we've got all kinds of natural gas, oil, and coal in the rest of the country."[23]

So much for "The Average English Canadian View", which Mr. Fisher claimed to represent, since that was the title of his speech.

CHAPTER FIVE
1962

INQUIRY

Much to the annoyance of the separatists, Mr. André Laurendeau, nationalist though he is, separatist though he once was, refuses to be of them. Still, he thinks, something must be done, and in the main editorial for the January 20 *Devoir*, he makes his New Year proposal: an inquiry on bilingualism to be carried out by the federal government. An over-all approach is needed, Mr. Laurendeau asserts, warning that bilingual cheques would be too little and too late. The warning goes unheeded, it is true, but it is there.

In the Commons Mr. Diefenbaker is asked whether the government is considering an inquiry on bilingualism.

"No", he says. Or "NO"! as it sounds in some Quebec ears.

"Mr. Diefenbaker *Pourquoi non?* (Why 'no'?)", protests Mr. Laurendeau on the front page of the January 24 *Devoir*. And he suspects the Prime Minister of "English Separatism".

At this point, Mr. Tommy Douglas, our New Democratic Party leader, thinks separatism is Canada's most important problem.

TOO LITTLE AND TOO LATE

"After Eight Years of Annual Debates, Ottawa Announces, the Cheques Will Be Bilingual", reads *Le Devoir* main front-page headline for February 7. Under this, predictably, is another headline, "It's Too Little and Too Late", the one for Mr. Laurendeau's short, angry editorial.

"The Central State, once more, is the professor of separatism," he finishes.

"The cheques printed by the government represent our only major grievance," says Pierre Vigeant in February of 1958.

"It's too little and too late," says Mr. Laurendeau in February of 1962.

Three years (for we do not count 1958) is indeed a long time in a revolution.

French-Canadian Quebec has been having one.

English Canada has not been having one.

Had the bilingual cheques been granted in 1963 instead of 1962, there would in all probability have been public demonstrations against them, perhaps even riots; and the newspapers and the provincial government might well have been deluged with demands that all cheques that were not unilingual, and in the most impeccable French, be declared illegal.

It is in this fashion that the crisis between French and English Canada has intensified from year to year since 1959.

Dark Memories

If Mr. Laurendeau appears hard to please, it may help to remember that practically the whole of his public life has been filled with unfruitful attempts to come to satisfactory terms with the federal government. He gives us a pungent reminder of this fact in February 1962, when his book *La crise de la conscription, 1942 (The Conscription Crisis 1942)*, appears.[1]

The book hinges around the plebiscite of 1942 in which the government asked Canadians whether or not they would " 'consent to free the government from all obligations resulting from previous engagements restricting the methods of mobilization for military service?" '[2]

In other words, as French-Canadian nationalists saw it, the question was, would Canada let the government break its promise to French-Canadian Quebec that there would be no conscription for overseas service — a promise made originally in order to win Quebec's agreement to the decision to go to war?

It would indeed. The results of the plebiscite, proclaimed April 27, 1942, showed that Canadians had voted "YES" 63.7%, "NO", 36.3%. Quebec had voted "NO" 71.2%. The highest 'no' vote elsewhere was in the Yukon, with "NO" 31.7%.[3]

Mr. Laurendeau, intent upon the defense of his people, had campaigned intensively for "NO".

Summing it all up at the end of his book, the nationalist writes:

"There were two unequal forces present: we yielded. Through his art, Prime Minister King partially succeeded in masking the constraint. But there was constraint.

"During the war, many French-Canadian Quebecers felt they were living in an occupied country. The English were the occupying nation, the one that dictated conduct and prevented the national will from being effectively expressed; our politicians were the collaborationists. It was, compared with Hitler's Europe, a benign occupation; thanks to the moderation of King, the yoke remained supportable. We risked only our liberties, and even at that, the menace was rarely realized. But it is sufficient that it existed for life to be poisoned.

"That impression of having submitted to an occupation indicates to what point a large number of French Canadians then escaped, in their hearts and souls, from the bonds of the Central State. The greater the physical constraint, the less the moral adhesion and loyalty. To be sure, we respected the French-Canadian volunteers, because they risked their lives: but when, on the basis of the courage they manifested on the battle fields, we were asked to adhere to King's policies, we experienced a violent movement of recoil. Our hero would have been the conscript in revolt, the rebel . . . .

"After all, it was a question of sentiment, but one of them is self-respect. Moreover, the world is full of sentiments, and I wonder why the only one we should refuse to allow is the one we hold with respect to ourselves, and which is called the sentiment of human dignity."[4]

So ends the book.

"Dignity demands it (independence)" writes Marcel Chaput, "because, like those absent, minorities are always wrong".[5]

FREE CITY

One must not conclude too quickly that by 1962 all effective opposition to separatism has collapsed. There are still a sizable number of free-thinking individuals who have behind them years of resistance to popular enthusiasms and cure-alls of all descriptions.

Among these, Mr. Pierre-Elliot Trudeau comes to our attention in the April issue of *Cité Libre* (Free City), an intellectual little magazine[6] which is to see its sales rise sharply at this point due to its sole and exclusive subject for the month, Separatism. The major article is by Mr. Trudeau, who, with Gérard Pelletier, was the publication's co-editor.

In sum, Mr. Trudeau argues that separatism deludes those who subscribe to it with illusory promises of a better life; that it is vain, wasteful, and even positively harmful.

"All the time and all the energies that we use up in proclaiming the rights of our nationality, in invoking our providential mission, in bugling our virtues and in crying over our ancestors, in denouncing our enemies, and in declaring our independence, have never made one of our workers more skilled, one civil servant more competent, one financier more rich, one doctor more progressive, one bishop better educated, nor one of our politicians less illiterate. Nonetheless, if one excepts a few surly fellows, there's probably not one French-Canadian intellectual who hasn't discussed separatism at least four hours a week for a year; that makes how many thousands of two hundred hours spent exclusively in idle chatter? For who can say that he has heard, in all that time, a single argument that was not debated *ad nauseam* twenty years ago, forty years ago, sixty years ago ..." [7]

Elsewhere in the article Mr. Trudeau attacks not only the practicality but also the basic doctrines that lie behind separatism. For him, a sovereign Quebec would be undesirable, even if possible.

We may sum up Mr. Trudeau's ideas as follows: the separatist's comparisons between Quebec and recently-freed colonies is false; history shows that a country should not base itself upon a single religion, nation, or ideology, as to do so causes religious, national, or ideological wars; states must not, being imperfect, claim absolute sovereignty; man belongs to himself first of all and not to any particular race or language. Nationalism in French Canada has often made it value too highly all that distinguishes it from others, and resist all change, even progress, from the outside. A nationalistic government, Mr. Trudeau feels, is essentially intolerant, discriminatory, totalitarian. He believes that nationalism in either French or English Canada can destroy from within, causing death from asphyxiation, and that the promise of victory is to the one that renounces its nationalism to pursue broader, more humane ideals.

In June an entire book *Pourquoi je suis anti-séparatiste (Why I Am An Anti-Separatist)* by Jean-Charles Harvey,[8] appears to refute everything Dr. Chaput has said. In his eyes, too, the values of independence are chimerical.

"What are they offering us?" he asks in the first chapter, "Nothing." And he goes on with his exposition of his view that as Canadians French Canadians have everything they would have if Quebec were independent and a good deal more besides.

Both Mr. Trudeau and Mr. Harvey agree that, to a large extent, French Canada has had separatism thrust upon it, but they feel that this has occurred as a result of excessive English-Canadian nationalism which Quebec should not try to imitate. Mr. Harvey, moreover, has one very concrete suggestion for English Canadians who wish to satisfy French Canada's aspirations in a way that will dispose of the problem of separatism once and for all.

"The separatist idea would collapse in a day, I am sure, if the English-speaking provinces, forgetting the vain fears of the past, put an end to their tactics of Anglicization in the schools."

He quotes Mr. Louis A. Belisle, editor of the well-known French-Canadian dictionary.

'The most logical solution, to take advantage of the winds of independence that are blowing everywhere, would be this: demand a revision of the Constitution which would accord the French minorities, from one end of Canada to the other, advantages identical to those that Quebec has accorded to its English-speaking minorities."[9]

Separatism will hardly bring riches, according to University of Montreal economics professor André Reynaud, as *Cité Libre* returns to the attack in October. Quebec well knows and much resents that its per capita income is 28 percent lower than Ontario's. Professor Reynaud, however, believes that, with independence, the offending figure would be 50 percent instead of only 28 percent.

The new country would face trade barriers between it and the provinces, the necessity to try to balance its trade, a problem which now falls only on Ottawa, and the problem of trying to establish favourable tariff relationships with other, far more self-sufficient nations. Moreover, the economist lends no credence to the separatists' *vache à lait* concept of Quebec — the idea that the province, moronically docile, lets itself be milked by the rest of the country. Federal services, he says, are much cheaper than they would be if Quebec had to provide them itself. And Quebecers pay less federal income tax, per capita, than the national average, since their per capita income is 10 percent lower than the average for Canada. Finally, the unfavourable reaction that the new Quebec would surely draw from Americans and English Canadians could spell ruin as they own nearly all the factories and mines.

Since separatists treat non-separatists as "traitors", Professor Reynaud feels that he must conclude by offering French Canadians something positive. Let the provincial government deal with English Canada, he urges; and let us lose no energy in separatist agitation, but let us concentrate on the more pressing internal problems of education and economic planning.

COMPULSORY FATUITY

Comment on abrutit nos enfants (How They Make Our Children Stupid), by journalists Solange and Michel Chalvin,[10] arrives in May for the further enlightenment of society. Two years after *Frère Untel* there is, of course, no question about *whether* the schools are making children stupid or not. Realizing, however, that some parents may still be none too clear about the actual pedagogy of the process, the Chalvins undertake to remedy this deficiency: the key to it all, they explain, lies in the textbooks.

To begin with (all the following ideas are those of the Chalvins only and do not necessarily represent the views of the author), there is an excess of religious books, and not enough dealing with geography and the natural sciences. In addition, too many worn-out clichés, racism, false and lyrical patriotism, puerile and insignificant language, errors of language, sadism, the choice of mediocre authors, and word-for-word repetition of exercises and lessons from one year to another are some (not all) of the defects found in nearly all the texts and manuals.[11]

Thus the assault of the Chalvins. Since they are in the mainstream of the revolution, we may expect some radical changes in Quebec's school books.

THE MONEY MAKER

While various explanations have been offered for the Social Credit wave that swept over most of the province in the federal elections of June 18, 1962, everyone seems to agree that the importance of Mr. Réal Caouette was great indeed. If we may assume (which is not at all sure) that he did not attract votes through sheer force of televised mesmerism, then what he said must have had something to do with it all. Fortunately, we still have a record of some of his campaign speeches, the book, *Réal Caouette vous parle (Réal Caouette Talks to You)*,[12] having been published shortly after the elections in question. It claims to reproduce in print recordings of Mr. Caouette's 1962 speeches.

In the spring of 1962, the separatists have not yet satiated the revolution's appetite for cure-alls. The better to study the sovereign remedy offered by *les créditistes*, we may consider the following statement by Mr. Caouette:

"We must use the Bank of Canada for the credit necessary to the development of our natural resources. We have in Canada competent engineers, we have sociologists, we have tradesmen, we have journeymen, we have workmen, we have a whole people who can act, who can contribute, who can work to develop our natural resources.

"No one ever asks, to build a bridge, to build a highway, if we have the workmen available, if we have the materials available, if we have the contractors available, if we have the engineers available? No, it's always a question of where we are going to get the money to realize these projects, to realize these constructions." . . .[13]

"What is stopping us from developing our resources? We have nearly a million unemployed in Canada. The economists say there will be one million, two hundred thousand this winter. It will be the most abject misery, black misery everywhere, next winter.

"Why don't we develop our iron ore riches in Ungava? Why don't we develop our nickel mines, our copper mines, all our forests, all our natural resources ourselves? Why don't we do it by using the Bank of Canada? Isn't that bank there to serve the Canadian people! Let the bank render possible the establishment here of a steel mill that would finish the raw product, so that we can ourselves get on with the construction of Canadian automobiles, at home in Canada. But oh no! We have American automobiles, and in Canada, we have no special make of car, built exclusively in Canada."[14]

The great root of all evil, then, is lack of money, and the miraculous remedy (once *les créditistes* take office, of course) is the Bank of Canada.

If the Bank of Canada is the cure-all, what dark power is responsible for the present sorry state of affairs? Where will Social Credit find its universal villain and scapegoat? The answer is not far to seek:

". . . we see, unhappily, people who look after provincial, municipal, school or even federal administrations going to the financiers of the entire world to obtain permission for the Canadian people to develop its natural resources or to obtain permission for it to carry out various work projects in its own country.

"Is there anything more nonsensical, more stupid than to go and ask permission of New York to develop our iron ore in Ungava, in the Province of Quebec?

"Is there a method more stupid than to go to Chicago or London or Paris to ask for financial permission to develop our natural riches? . . .[15]

"Ladies and gentlemen, instead of the Mayor of Montreal geting down on his knees in New York to borrow a hundred million and more, why doesn't he go to the Federal Government, to the Federal Parliament . . . which would order the Bank of Canada to finance the Montreal *métro* — for a hundred million dollars at half of one percent — covering just the cost of administration". . . .[16]

Why is not all well in Canada and in the Province of Quebec? Because, say the Creditors, we are dependent upon the great financial powers of New York, London, Paris, because we have to beg permission of them before we can do anything; because we are "in tutelage", as Dr. Chaput would say.

To Mr. Caouette, the cure-all, the key to glorious freedom and independence is the Bank of Canada; to Dr. Chaput, it is the sovereignty of Quebec.

To Mr. Caouette, the nasty ogre that won't let Quebecers do as they please, that humiliates them and makes them come begging for permission like children, is High (and foreign) Finance; to Dr. Chaput it is Anglo-Saxon Canada as represented by the Federal Government.

If Social Credit in Quebec presents the same basic pattern as separatism, Mr. Caouette goes the separatists one better in that he offers not only the economic liberty of their province (to a Creditor money is *the* standard; economic liberty, therefore, means Liberty, unlimited), but also personal liberty. After all, a *créditiste* might argue, what makes a man a prisoner of circumstances, subservient, dependent, subject to all kinds of pressures, forced to practically beg for his daily bread; in short, what makes a man a mouse if it is not lack of money in his pockets?

But the dismal government (federal or provincial, what's the difference? Mr. Caouette argues) keeps taking all our money, insidiously, a little more all the time, in taxes to pay for all its plans, its insurance, its pensions, etc. . . .:

"It's not plans, Ladies and Gentlemen, that the people need, that the families need, that we need. What we need in Canada is security, yes, but not to the detriment of personal liberty. But when will we have liberty with security? We have liberty with security when we have buying power in our pockets so that we can order what we need, so that we can decide ourselves what is necessary, and we don't need a government to decide in our place or to choose in our place."[17]

We don't, he might have said, need a government to keep us *en tutelle,* like children.

Social Credit would seem to have much appeal for those who, affected by the revolution, feel that the *status quo* is unendurable, but who do not hate the Anglo-Saxons or Canada, and are very likely most concerned by the problems of day-to-day financing. Since the Social Credit villain is High Finance, it perhaps has a special appeal to people who feel resentful because they are in debt, particularly if they are charged high interest rates. On the other hand, since Mr. Caouette repeatedly talks in terms of Canada, he may fail to arouse those of separatist tendencies who prefer to restrict their attention to Quebec.

Later, of course, in 1963, the federal Social Creditors are to split into the Thompson and Caouette factions, and the latter is to set its sails as best it can to get the full benefit of separatist winds.

By the time of the elections, the population of Quebec has been subjected, by such notables as the Abbés Dion and O'Neill, Brother Anonymous, Dr. Chaput, the Chalvins and many more, to nearly three years of reports, articles, and books about the utter worthlessness of its present situation. All of these have contributed to the generalized feeling that the Social Credit slogan, *Vous n'avez rien à perdre* ("You have nothing to lose") is really true.

MASTERS IN OUR HOUSE

September 1962, saw the appearance of *Devoir* editor Paul Sauriol's book, *La nationalisation de l'électricité (The Nationalization of Electric Power).*[18] Prefaced by the Minister of Natural Resources, the Honourable René Lévesque, it is dedicated to arguments in favour of the title project.

Shortly thereafter, the government announces that elections are to be held because the nationalization of electric power, which it proposes to carry out, is too big an undertaking to be ventured upon without the support of the people. Foremost among those advocating the plan are René Lévesque in the cabinet and Paul Sauriol, who, aside from his book, dedicates many editorials to the subject in *Le Devoir.*

The Union Nationale does not take an unequivocal stand on the question, preferring to argue that the total performance of the government must be judged and that the electricity issue could be settled by plebiscite.

"*Maîtres chez nous*" (Masters In Our House), the Liberal slogan for the campaign, again may give us a sense of returning to familiar scenes if we have read Dr. Chaput's book, previously discussed. It contains the following passages:

"The world is made of separatists. The man who is master of his house is a separatist ... To progress, the French Canadians must be masters in their house ... Exactly as you have the right and even the duty to be the master of your house, without hate or injustice for your neighbour, French Canada has the right and the duty to be master of its house, without manifesting hostility or doing harm to English Canada."[19]

Officially, however, the separatists remain a miniscule and crackpot minority, in the eyes of the government.

Returning to the nationalization of electric power, the principal reason for it, as seen by Mr. Sauriol, is that it is necessary to "our economic independence and to planned development of our industry".[20]

In the general picture, hydro-electric energy is of paramount importance in a number of provinces, Canada being second only to the United States in this area. Quebec, with the lowest electricity rates in the world, is in this respect the most favoured of the provinces, and is richer than they are in easily-harnessed sources of hydro-electric power.[21]

Nevertheless, Mr. Sauriol argues, under private control the distribution of electricity is poor and inefficient. The regions of Abitibi and Gaspé are inadequately served.[22] In general, there is "foolish, ruinous waste".[23]

Given the ever-growing nationalism of the time, one of the strongest of the editor's arguments concerns the federal taxes imposed upon the private electricity companies. Nationalization of electricity is to save Quebec nearly twenty million dollars a year on that score alone.

Quebec's eagerness to retrieve all the money it possibly can in this way is made infinitely keener by its belief that the Federal Government already has far more than its share of all taxes.

"... For the last twenty years the central government has been conducting a campaign for fiscal centralization, at the expense of the provinces.

"Over a fifteen-year period, Quebec has consistently struggled to obtain a more equitable share of the income tax which Ottawa began to seize on such a large scale during the war. . . .

"We are letting tens of millions of dollars slip through our fingers, millions we could easily recover. And no revolution is required: the example has been set by other provinces, particularly Ontario. Unlike Quebec, the other provinces have no objection to federal grants in provincial fields such as education; they have no need to protect their fiscal system to defend a religious and cultural minority; they do not feel their rights encroached upon by Ottawa's fiscal and constitutional acts of aggression."[24]

Of no less importance than the federal taxes is the fact that the electricity companies are not, to any extent, under French-Canadian ownership. Although Mr. Sauriol believes that the nationalization would be necessary even if this were not true,[25] he is not one to minimize the importance of "Economic Colonialism".[26]

Quebec, like the rest of Canada, is having its natural resources developed chiefly by American capital. Moreover, the Canadian capital that is invested in Quebec is "for the most part also foreign, since it is mainly English-Canadian Capital".[27]

With respect to the whole of Canada, electrical resources are for the most part exploited by Canadian capital. Yet in Quebec, the province with the greatest hydro-electric potential, this capital is nearly all American or English Canadian.[28]

"Quebec, French Canada's national state, is an underdeveloped country; the profits of its rapidly expanding economy benefit outsiders, and only the crumbs fall to us.

"The remarks are particularly relevant to electricity . . ." [29]

Is the nationalization of electric power revolutionary? Mr. Sauriol, a man of mature years, would answer no, as would many of those who favoured the undertaking. It could be and was argued that the nationalization was but a natural step in a process of evolution that was sufficiently protracted in any case.

Whether or not it is revolutionary, the nationalization certainly serves the purposes of the revolution. To the extent that it liberates Quebec from "foreign", that is, non-French-Canadian finance, it has an appeal comparable to that of Mr. Caouette when he says that Quebec doesn't have to borrow from New York, London or Paris. To the extent that it liberates Quebec from the impositions of the Federal Government, it has the same appeal as separatism.

INDUSTRIAL PAROCHIALISM?

Almost exactly a year after Mr. Douglas Fisher had presented his powerfully-built person in Quebec City, at Laval's Congress on Canadian affairs, to tell everyone just how essential, in his "average English-Canadian view" was Quebec in the scheme of things, steel-driving Mr. Donald Gordon spoke up to prove that a railway does not necessarily join East and West after all.

Appearing in the Commons to report on the operation of the enterprise he manages, that is the federally-owned Canadian National Railways, Mr. Gordon was asked by *créditiste* Mr. Gilles Grégoire why, out of the company's twenty-eight top directors, not one was French Canadian. In reply, Mr. Gordon reportedly said that there were not enough qualified French Canadians available, and that so long as he was president no one would be given a job just because he was French Canadian.

Mr. Gordon has repeatedly protested that he is not anti-French Canadian and that press reports to the contrary, he did not make statements prejudicial to French Canadians at this time. To be fair to both Mr. Gordon and his critics, we reproduce the official record of the questions and comments in the "Appendix" below.

It is interesting to compare French-Canadian reaction to Mr. Gordon's statement with that evoked by Mr. Fisher a year earlier.

Mr. Fisher, as will be recalled, had told Quebec plainly just what it could do with its cherished independence and (as he saw them) unduly elevated ideas about its own importance and worth. How, then, can we explain the absence of any really violent manifestations in consequence?

That the revolution was a year younger, and that much less inclined to violence, when Mr. Fisher spoke than when Mr. Gordon did, is no doubt part of the answer. It is not, however, the principal part, which latter is not quite so simple.

Mr. Fisher did not arouse enmity because he was looked upon as honest. In French-Canadian nationalist eyes, he was just what he said he was: a representative "average English Canadian", a typical English-Canadian separatist. (By "English-Canadian separatist", the French Canadian does not necessarily mean someone who advocates separatism. Usually he means someone whose thinking leaves so little place for French Canadians that he forces separatism upon them.) While he may have made some French Canadians swallow rather hard, they felt that in him they were simply coming to grips with harsh reality. English Canada? This was it, and there was nothing you could do about it.

"We like him better than many of your flattering *bonne-ententistes*," was the average French-Canadian view. "A few of them may be sincere, but others are just trying to sugar the pill, the better to keep us in a position of inferiority and (or) assimilate us. Your Mr. Fisher throws no bouquets but at least you know where you're at with him. He probably can't help it. After all, it's not his fault if he's an average English Canadian."

With Mr. Gordon it was different. Not only was he guilty, French Canadians believed, of telling them in effect that he despised them and had no use for them; he also manifested (so they thought) flagrant arrogance and injustice towards them. Hence the demonstrations, the near-riots, the burning in effigy.

Mr. Fisher, after all, was a delegate of Port Arthur. Mr. Gordon, as president of a federal corporation, was responsible to all Canadians, French-speaking, English-speaking, and others.

TAKE IT OR LEAVE IT

In December of 1962, Dr. Marcel Chaput founded his *Parti républicain du Québec,* the first provincial political party to have the independence of Quebec as its first and major, if not only goal.

Also in December, Premier Lesage made his first and final offer to the electricity companies that were to be nationalized. It was take it or leave it, with the courts to decide in the latter case.

Shawinigan protested that the offer was too low. Shawinigan was the largest of the corporations involved and for a time it looked as if quite a battle might shape up.

The Premier stood his ground, reiterating the final nature of his proposal.

Shawinigan took it.

CHAPTER SIX
1963

By the beginning of 1963, the winds of the revolution were not yet at hurricane force.

In January, Mr. Jean Lesage, Premier of Quebec said that it was Confederation's last chance. Mr. Gérard Filion left *Le Devoir* to take over as head of the General Investment Corporation, a government organization designed to pool available investment funds to buy shares in Quebec industries.

In February, the Progressive Conservative government resigned.

March 8 saw the beginning of violence, later to be attributed to a score of young terrorists calling themselves the Quebec Liberation Front (FLQ or *Front de la libération québecoise*). On March 14, *Le Devoir* reported that the French revolutionary song "*Ça ira*" had been sung amidst the applause greeting the decision of the *Rasssemblement pour l'indépendance nationale* (RIN) to become a political party. In the same paper, the director of the RIN organ *l'Indépendance*, Pierre Bourgault, was reported to have said that independence is useless without the revolution.

April 5 witnessed Mr. Lesage's fiscal ultimatum: within a year Quebec must be granted twenty-five per cent of the income tax on individuals and companies and all of the inheritance taxes.

April 8 saw a marked decline in the fortunes of Mr. Diefenbaker and Mr. Caouette as the federal elections took place.

While the Conservative's fate caused little surprise (some Quebecers were surprised that the provincial Tories did as well as they did), the cooling of *créditiste* enthusiasm left nearly everyone puzzled.

Possibly it was just that Social Credit had already been tried and found wanting. It was almost a year since the previous federal elections. A year is a long time in a revolution. Since the Creditors had not, in that time, made anyone much richer, perhaps they were simply written off. In addition, Social Credit has powerful enemies. Foremost among them, as we've seen, is Labour chief Jean Marchand. Premier Lesage denounced Social Credit on April 5.

The press is generally against it. And, true or false, Mr. Caouette's bitter assertion that the Liberals had been supported by American finance is also significant.

April 20 marked the death of the first FLQ victim.

On May 11, Dr. Guy Marcoux, one of Social Credit's leading figures in Quebec, resigned.

On May 17, the storm reached a climax as five bombs exploded in the mailboxes of Westmount.

The bombs were designed to set English against French Canadians. Let us now, however, examine a situation that involves the Quebec Government alone. This is the one created by the low, flat imitation-factory known as the twentieth-century school.

ORGANIZED CONFUSION

In a broad, general way, Quebec's educational problems compare with those of the rest of North America. The number of teachers and pupils in the province has doubled in the last fifteen years — evidence that here, as elsewhere, children are staying in school much longer than before, and that in any case their numbers have increased substantially. Here as elsewhere we have the scientific and industrial revolution and a society that has become largely urban over the last century (in 1871 Quebec was seventy-seven per cent rural in its population and twenty-three per cent urban. Now it is seventy-five per cent urban and twenty-five per cent rural).[1] Since the system or systems which attempt to cope with the situation have not been greatly revised, either in their methods or general philosophy, for at least a hundred years, it is not surprising that ever-more pressing questions concerning the schools and universities have been of major importance in the politics of 1963.

Aroused by cries of anguish and frustration from Brother Anonymous and a host of others, the government established a Royal Commission of Inquiry on Education in the spring of 1961. This was (and is) the Parent Commission, which acts under the chairmanship of the Right Reverend Alphonse Marie Parent, p.a., Vice-Rector of Quebec City's Laval University. In April of 1963, the Commission presented Part One of its Report, "The Structure of the Educational System at the Provincial Level". Immediately, the government prepared legislation based upon the Commission's recommendations.

To understand the government bill and the various reactions it has evoked, we must first consider the present state of affairs as described by the Commission.

Some of the Parent Commission's general criticisms of educational forms help to explain why an inquiry was necessary in the first place. We read, for example, that "three serious defects in school administration prevent the government from exercising its educational functions effectively". We must note, here, that the Commission is assuming that the government has educational functions. There are still those who maintain that pure Mademoiselle Education and that notorious rake Politics must be kept strictly apart, or, if this proves impossible, that they must never be allowed to see each other except in the presence of the strictest of chaperones. Analyzing the "defects", the Report goes on, "the first springs from the fragmentation of the school system. Different authorities govern the private institutions, the schools operated by the Ministry of Youth, and the public schools; the Roman Catholic and Protestant sectors of the public system are autonomous; a wall divides the colleges and universities from the primary, secondary and normal schools." Where the government has control, the system is split "betwen several ministries, each managing its own schools and determining its curricula without co-ordination or over-all planning." Finally, the recruitment of personnel in the Department of Education "is almost invariably restricted to those sectors under the Department's immediate control and is in competition with school commissions able to offer higher salaries . . ." [2]

Because of the complex history of education in the Province "it is not surprising to find a certain incoherence, and frequent contradictions, in a body of law gradually formulated over a period of more than a century. It takes much patience and deep study to work one's way through this maze of separate Acts and their subsequent amendments."[3]

Without aspiring to work through the "maze", we may examine the salient features of Quebec's main educational structures. Perhaps the first useful distinction one can make is between the public and private schools. In both areas there is a clean split between Roman Catholic and Protestant schools, with, in the private sector, a few non-confessional schools and some three hundred vocational schools. While for Protestants the private schools are of limited importance, they are crucial in the French and Roman Catholic area. Here the private classical colleges still offer the only preparation for some university faculties, and this in spite of the fact that the whole private sector takes care of only about 104,000 pupils, whereas the Roman Catholic public schools cope with over 1,030,-000 of them. Nevertheless, things are more democratic than they were when the classical colleges monopolized all the instruction that led to university. These colleges, with the odd exception, are directed by priests, nuns, or brothers, though forty per cent of their teachers are now lay people. Private interests still monopolize university training.[4]

Although it doesn't really do anything, the Council of Education is of key importance as we look into the public sector of education. It is composed of three equal parts: Roman Catholic bishops, Roman Catholic laymen, and Protestants. The bishops include all those in the province, and each is matched by one Catholic layman and one Protestant layman. Appointments to the Council are for life. It is presided over by the Superintendent, but he votes only on the Committee formed by those of his faith. The only specific authority given to the Council is to establish one or two committees composed of persons competent in pedagogy and in agricultural science to be entrusted with the preparation of a program of agricultural teaching in the Province. It has never established such committees. Between 1908 and 1960 the Council never met. When it met in 1960, the purpose was to celebrate the centenary of its creation. It met again in 1962 to adopt a brief for the Parent Commission.[5]

The Council of Education is, however, proof that the parts may be greater than the whole. The parts consist of the two Committees into which it is split: Catholic and Protestant. The Protestant one, being only half as big as the Catholic one, is possibly somewhat less clumsy. To these Committees is entrusted "the general direction and control of teaching, as well as the organization and educational discipline in all public schools, in normal schools and in various home economics institutes".[6]

Thus the Committees look after textbooks, programs, teachers' qualifications, standards for school buildings, the length of the school year, and other matters. As to their efficiency, the Parent Commission points out that many of their members have other important functions. Each group meets in plenary session only four times a year. To assist it, therefore, the Roman Catholic Committee employs the services of a large complex of commissions, sub-commissions, and sub-committees, and the Protestant Committee operates in a similar, if somewhat less intricate fashion.

It is observed that while the Catholic Commission can call upon many specialists, questions are handled in such a many-staged, complex manner that the responsibility for what, if anything, is eventually decided cannot be pinned down to those responsible. The Protestant Committee, however, has apparently adopted a program of study in accord with the needs of the children.[7]

While the Committees' decisions are subject to Cabinet approval, the Parent Commission complains that the Government cannot really exercise its authority because the questions are too complex and there is no responsible minister. There is no true "articulation" between the two Committees and the Government.[8]

A difficulty inherent in having the public schools under only two committees, one Catholic and the other Protestant, must be immediately evident to anyone who can conceive of a creature which is (a) human, (b) non-Catholic, (c) non-Protestant, or (d) Catholic or Protestant but opposed to the idea that public schools should segregate children according to the private beliefs of their parents. With the freedom of expression, and the eagerness to exploit it that has characterized Quebec since the death of the Chief, a number of people are saying openly that they can conceive of just that. Consequently, while *Le Mouvement laïque de la langue française* — MLF (The French-language Lay Movement), an organization in favour of neutral public schools, has not yet produced revolutionary results it will bear watching.

At present, French-speaking parents who do not wish to send their children to schools under the Catholic Committee usually have to enroll them in English-language schools. When a French-speaking Protestant appears on the horizon, the majority of Quebecers may witness the phenomenon but many don't quite believe it. They are shocked by ideas such as those put forth by the MLF. The MLF, on the other hand, is perhaps even more shocked by the conditions imposed upon its adherents and sympathizers.

An example of this latter type of feeling is given by Mrs. Therèse-Gouin-Decarie who spoke to the MLF Congress of November 4 and 5, 1961, on the psychological aspects of having children in a school that teaches a religion other than that of their parents:

"The most tragic cases are those of the children of French-Canadian parents who have become agnostic — for this is pure aberration. Our society accepts the fact that the French, the Jews, and the English may become unbelievers and yet maintain moral standards, but it is a contradiction in terms to say that a French Canadian may be agnostic and moral."

Returning to the present situation, we find that in addition to the two-Committee Council of Education, there is also the Department of Education. Composed of the Superintendent and two secretaries plus various lesser luminaries. The Department has rather vague, over-all duties. According to the Parent Commission, it acts as the executive branch of the Committees. If at times it fails to shine in this role, this may be due to the fact that it operates in "small, over-crowded offices scattered in various parts of the City of Quebec" which "make it difficult for officials to consult files, and an elaborate messenger service is required to carry records from office to office. . . ."[9]

Completing the system, we have the school corporations; they build and maintain schools, engage personnel, and levy taxes. They must now have their budgets approved by the Minister of Youth, and must have authorization from the Departments of Youth and Municipal Affairs when they wish to borrow. The Minister of Youth also decides how much government money shall be spent to repair and construct schools.

Quebec does have, in addition, a number of institutes of technology and other specialized institutes dealt with by special acts and administered by a variety of departments, including those of Youth, Family and Social Welfare, Labour, Health, Agriculture, Game and Fisheries, Lands and Forests, Industry and Commerce, Natural Resources, and the Attorney General.[10]

As is apparent in the foregoing, the Parent Commission is highly critical of existing arrangements, chiefly because of their fragmented nature and the government's powerlessness to co-ordinate them. Its first recommendation is that a Minister of Education be appointed "whose function shall be to promote and coordinate educational services at all levels, including the private and public sectors".[11] This does not mean, however, that the Commission is prepared simply to turn everything over to the government. To make sure that there is no mistake about this, it also recommends the creation of an independent sixteen-member Superior Council of Education, which is not merely to advise the Minister but "to give its judgment on all questions which the Minister is obliged to submit to it, namely: teaching programmes, examination standards, and official diplomas; qualifying standards for teaching personnel; plans for locating and establishing educational institutions. . . ."[12] In other words, the Superior Council is to keep an eye on the Minister. It is to be appointed by the Cabinet, but its President and Vice-President are to be one Catholic and the other Protestant.

Thus, the government, intent on being re-elected, would still have to wonder who is the most Catholic of the Catholics and the most Protestant of the Protestants, and try to get these people suitably placed on the Council.

The Minister in any case is not to have the initiative in matters concerning religion. There is still to be a Roman Catholic Committee and a Protestant Committee to make regulations in this area.

Since teachers, textbooks, programs, in fact everything about a school in some part affects, or may affect, its religious character, the Committees' mandate could be interpreted in a way which would make them as all-powerful as at present.

A third of the Catholic Committee is to be chosen by the assembled bishops of the Province, and the chairman of the Catholic Committee is to be chosen after consultation with the assembled bishops. The Protestant Committee also is to have church representatives.[13]

Thus, the Parent Commission, and the government's proposed legislation, known as Bill 60, which, as we have said, is based upon it, try to steer a middle road between complete government control and no government control. For the sake of efficiency, the Report and Bill 60 give education to the government; for the sake of the religious interests, they leave it in the hands of the churches. Not surprisingly, they have aroused considerable opposition in both areas, and Bill 60 is still awaiting action despite Youth Minister Gérin-Lajoie's confidence, enthusiasm, and vigorous summer-and-fall campaigns in favour of it. Until September, 1963, the government seemed determined to implement Bill 60 with hardly any delay at all. Then the bishops suggested certain amendments. Since then the government's position has been one of diplomatic retreat, or perhaps more accurately, one of assurance that it had never really advanced anyway.

In sum, with amendments largely in line with the bishops' recommendations, it passed the Assembly (February 6, 1964) and was presented to Quebec's Union National-dominated Upper House, which also passed it after making a few amendments of its own. The effect of all these amendments is to restrict the power of the new ministry and leave the Protestant and Catholic Committees in a position to control curriculum almost, if not quite as much as they have in the past. With Bill 60 the conservative, counter-revolutionary forces of the province mark up ten points — temporarily, at least. For Premier Lesage has rejected two of the Legislative Council's amendments and the battle will go on until one side backs down.*

Bombarding Bill 60 from opposite directions, we find the Jesuit magazine *Relations* of November 1963 and the same month's *Cité Libre*. Praising the bishops' amendments, *Relations* affirms that the bishops request the respect of the fundamental rights of children, parents and teachers, thus suggesting a remedy "much more profound and apt to assure peace in the schools than that which Bill 60 claims to realize by falling back on the very old and too easy solution of putting everything into the hands of the State".[14]

Relations sums up the position of the bishops as follows: "that in Quebec a system of education be built which will permit every child, no doubt to learn, but also to develop his own personality to the maximum, and in all its dimensions, including the religious one". To this end the bishops are held to desire that parents be allowed to choose the schools they deem best for their children, without financial penalty, and that, to safeguard this principle, all institutions that satisfy the general norms of the State be accorded equal legal, academic, and financial treatment.

In sharp contrast, *Cité Libre*'s Maurice Blain boldly puts forth the claims of Caesar:

"Neither the Church nor the State appear to have realized the basic essentials of the lay position, without which every arrangement is but hollow deception:

"That in the field of general, earthly welfare, which includes that of education, the sovereignty of the State is higher than that of the Churches;

"That the Churches have no special privileges in public teaching;

"That the State must respect the freedom of conscience of its citizens, the believers and the non-believers, and for this reason it must guarantee their freedom to choose their religious teaching;

"That finally, in the exercise of religious liberty in State schools, the Churches, guardians of the faith of their followers, but not of citizens' rights, are only collaborators of the State".[15]

An interesting characteristic of the Parent Report and Bill 60 is the willingness to mark time that they reflect, the knowledge on the part of those who support them that they embody no sacred principles, and that their offerings will be valid for a limited time only. No knights in armour charge to the defense of Bill 60. Pre-

---

* With predictable compromise, Bill 60 became law on March 19.

senting the case for it in his recent book *Pourquoi le bill 60? (Why Bill 60)*[16] Youth Minister Gérin-Lajoie feels it necessary to include the following reservation:

"We must warn our successors that there's no question of sacred, unalterable principles, endowed with their independent existence, but of practical, provisional measures, drawn up by a society at a particular point in course of its development. To fabricate new myths from Bill 60 and its propositions would be a regrettable error."[16]

The old myths, incidentally, as seen by Mr. Gérin-Lajoie, are as follows: the myth of survival — the belief that what has saved French Canada will always save it; the myth of gratitude — the clergy deserves full confidence for having saved French Canada in spite of itself; the myth that politics are bad for education; and the myth that only the elite has a certain education and is able to transmit it. Attached to this is the belief that education is not for the masses.[17]

In French-Canadian philosophy, it is often held that only Anglo-Saxons will stoop to such matter-of-fact expediency and compromise as is embodied in Bill 60. The Latin spirit, in contrast, is thought to turn instinctively towards some ideal, some Universal Truth whenever it has a problem to solve.

Pressure in favour of religiously neutral schools will quite likely increase. Recently the Honourable Guy Favreau, Minister of Citizenship and Immigration,* pointed out that, under the Constitution, Quebec could have its own immigration policy and should, in his opinion, give active encouragement to potential French-speaking immigrants. Commenting, Dr. Jacques Mackay, President of the MLF, congratulated the federal government on its policy but argued that the lack of neutral schools in the province discourages many immigrants and would-be immigrants. "We know", he said recently "the difficulties with the schools that beset some sixty thousand French-speaking new Canadians living in Montreal. Many of them being non-Catholic or Catholic but hostile to the denominational school, it is difficult for them to send their children to the present schools, and at great inconvenience they often resort to private institutions. We know that, each year, a certain number of them prefer to return to their country of origin." *(Le Devoir Dec.* 20, 1963).

* Now Federal Minister of Justice.

In the main *Devoir* editorial for December 24, Mr. André Laurendeau writes under the heading "The Event of the Year in French Canada", and chooses the government's proposal to create a minister of education as his title subject. While admitting all the difficulties, hesitations, and large question marks still so intimately associated with the plan, Mr. Laurendeau believes that "We have crossed the Rubicon. The solutions will be more or less frank, rapid, and generous, but we can't imagine a retreat. The machine is in motion, despite all the braking of ideologists and self-centered financiers. We are leaving one epoch and entering another, even if we don't know exactly how quickly the change will take place or how far it will go."

BOUQUET

The summer of 1963 sees more awareness of what is taking place in Quebec but not a complete abandonment, by any means, of the head-in-sand position. Though FLQ explosions reverberate in the news services of the world, there is still no lack of English-speaking Canadians who believe there's nothing wrong that a little law and order won't clear up, that you can muddle through without really waking up at all.

Typical of this attitude is a commentary in *The Chatham Daily News*, quoted by the *Quebec Chronicle-Telegraph* on June 28 under the heading "Bouquet for the Province". *The Chatham Daily* is quoted as follows on the subject of Quebec terrorism:

"Canadians were concerned at the increasing extent of the actual lawlessness, concerned at the peril of the contagion spreading, and getting out of hand, and menacing Confederation itself."

The *News* cannot understand how those wonderful, efficient Quebec police could have been criticized for the methods they used in arresting and locking up the suspects:

". . . some strident editors who had no words of thanks to the Quebec authorities for their efficient service to our common country, went out of their way to berate the Quebec authorities for their handling of their problem, for such items as disregard of Habeas Corpus, refusal of bail, and violation of the Federal Bill of Rights."

So Canadians, at this point, *were* concerned! Past tense: *were*. And of course the police are completely justified in not worrying about the basic rights of their suspects, not when the *News* is interested only in efficiency! If Mr. Laurendeau is called upon to back up his Negro King editorial, he could point to such articles.

Let us return to reality. "Could", you can almost hear the *News* ask in a hurt, unbelieving tone, "— Could that horrible, nationalistic French *Devoir* deal with reality?"

In *Le Devoir* of July 5, the anonymous columnist *"Isocrate"* gives us his idea of "P.P." efficiency.

"Blundering should be avoided at all costs ... The stupidity that should have been avoided was to place artificially on the heads of the FLQ dynamiters the halo of heroism and martyrdom they did not have. Now they have it. Listen to the conversations. Read the weekend papers. The youthfulness of the terrorists, their good upbringing, their position as the sons of good families did not, by themselves, change the current of opinion. Through the good graces of a police force suddenly become just as heavily clumsy as it had been lamentably slow, the odious nature of the terrorist provocation has been transferred to the guardians of public order."

In the following day's *Devoir* *"Isocrate"* writes:

"Leaving aside the madmen at liberty because of the insufficiency of our psychiatric services, there are, besides the recent FLQ culprits, victims, to various degrees, of patriotic illuminism, who are already engaged — and who are making military preparations — to stage the Battle of the Plains of Abraham again with the opposite results. There are not many, it is true, but they are as ardent as they are disinterested. In their revolutionary mysticism, they know that there will be victims. They have chosen to be among them. Not necessarily to fight an army and three combined police forces. But to 'stimulate' the separatist chiefs, to strain the situation, to intimidate the responsible politicians, and to manipulate public opinion. There will be other explosions, other attacks, other threats. . . ."

Even if *"Isocrate"* were wrong about the new crop of terrorists, it would still be true that, at the time he wrote at least, little or nothing had been done to make further violence unlikely.

BIG GAME

So are they all, all honourable men

❋ ❋ ❋

I will not do them wrong, I rather choose
To wrong the dead, to wrong myself and you,
Than I will wrong such honourable men.

Shakespeare (*Julius Caesar*)

More savage, more total in its condemnation of the powers that be — provincial powers, that is — than any book previously produced by the revolution, is *J'accuse les assassins de Coffin*[18] *(I Accuse Coffin's Assassins)*, written by *Editions du Jour* editor, Jacques Hébert.* In order to appreciate his efforts, we must recall something that happened ten years ago in the light in which Mr. Hébert appears to see it.

In the early days of June, 1953, three hunters from Pennsylvania, Eugene Lindsey, his son Richard, and the latter's friend Frederick Claar, ventured into the depths of Quebec's Gaspé Peninsula, loaded for bear. Everything suggested that the bears would have no more luck than is usual in such circumstances, for the hunters' weaponry was up to the usual high standards. As man and beast stalked cautiously in the shadow of the bush, studying each other's moves, there is every reason to believe that the hands stroking the rifle stocks were steady, that the lips covering the comparatively small, harmless teeth wore a smile of confidence and anticipation, and that the eyes above those lips were clear and quick, not easily to be taken by surprise.

The bears didn't leave very much of their adversaries for the search party which arrived about a month later. It looked as though their victory had been complete, for while remains of all three hunters were eventually discovered, the bears appeared to have escaped unscathed. For a time, one might have wondered. Would anyone dare go hunting in the Gaspé after this? What calibre of rifle would be sufficient for the terrible bears of Gaspé?

Evidence soon appeared, however, to suggest that the hunters may have been quite adequately equipped to deal with bears. If these men had forgotten anything, it was that whether a man be on a crowded boulevard in the heart of Montreal, or alone in the most remote spot in Quebec's vast wilderness, there is only one creature that is really dangerous, only one whose bland approach and innocent appearance is never to be trusted, only one whose sudden, lethal assault is ever to be feared and guarded against in all circumstances.

Bears the hunters could cope with. They had forgotten about their fellow human beings.

Who had done the dire deed? What would become of the tourist industry? One can imagine the brief flurry of confusion, the ques-

* Formerly, Editor-in-Chief of Editions de l'Homme, Jacques Hébert formed his own publishing firm, Editions du Jour in 1961.

tions. Then the Province turned where, for years, it had always turned, listening as it had always listened, to the Boss, the Chief, the man who had never yet failed to speak and to act.

"Get him!" said Mr. Duplessis, or words to that effect. The culprit must be found.

Almost miraculously, everything changed. Where there had been disorder, confusion, the crack of that whip brought steely discipline. Where there had been indecision, the Voice brought swift, resolute action. Where there had been ignorance, men sprang forth who could have been torn to pieces before they would have admitted that every least detail of the Coffin murder case, as it came to be known, was not as crystal-clear to them as if they had been hovering over the scene of the crime, watching the murders from a helicopter as they were committed.

Caught in the vise of their omniscience was Wilbert Coffin, forty-one year-old Gaspé prospector; he spoke only English,[19] was descended from an old family of Empire Loyalists,[20] was an Anglican, had a common-law wife, had little money, and didn't run away. (One gathers that he was also somewhere in the general vicinity, somewhere in the province at least, when the bears discovered an unlooked for ally, or allies, in their maneuvers with Eugene Lindsey and Co.)

Beyond giving the briefest outline, it would serve no purpose to go into the grisly details of the case here. The reader may consult *The Coffin Murder Case* (Kingswood House, Toronto), a book by the *Toronto Daily Star*'s John Edward Belliveau, of which Mr. Hébert thoroughly approves. There is, of course, Mr. Hébert's 1958 book, *Coffin était innocent (Coffin Was Innocent)*, and his present one, which is in question here. It is enough to say that Coffin spent about two and a half years in the psychological torture chamber of the death cell while his friends and foes tugged for possession of the rope. The latter won the struggle on February 10, 1956.

Shooting tourists can give a province a bad name and even interfere with its tourist revenue. Mr. Hébert's theory is that a culprit had to be found, and found fast, or the Boss would get really angry. The book implies that his men, knowing his temper and finding in Mr. Coffin an available, unwary, and relatively defenseless suspect, decided to get it over with and fell upon the hapless prospector with one accord.

Mr. Duplessis' insistence upon quick action was reinforced, according to Mr. Hébert, by American pressures which found expression in a number of ways. There were the tourists, especially as represented by the Pennsylvania Federation of Sportsmen's Clubs (200,000 members, all free to spend their vacation money in Quebec or elsewhere), Pennsylvania Congressman James E. Van Zandt, the American Consul at Quebec, the State Department, and John Foster Dulles.

As far as the revolution is concerned, it is not the murder case itself that is important and the alleged misconduct of the procedures concerning it, but the accusation of legal murder that Mr. Hébert is making against a number of men who are, here and now, among the Province's most honoured and imposing pillars of justice and order. What Mr. Duplessis may have done or left undone is one thing. But if, as Mr. Hébert alleges, the death of an innocent man was brought about through grave dereliction of duty on the part of the late premier and those who represented the law of the land in Quebec, and if these latter men still represent the law in this part of Canada, changes of government notwithstanding, then that is quite another thing. For the big game that Mr. Hébert is tracking includes the Honourable Antoine Rivard, then Attorney-General, now a judge on the Court of Queen's Bench, the Honourable Noél Dorion, Secretary of State and President of the Privy Council under Diefenbaker, the Honourable Paul Miquelon, Superior Court judge, the Honourable George Blanchard, District Court judge (Rimouski), Captain Alphonse Matte, now Inspector-General of Quebec's Provincial Police, and Mr. Charles Edouard Cantin, Assistant to the Attorney-General.

Mr. Hébert's theory is that evidence which would have tended to clear Coffin was concealed or passed over, and that half-truth, distortion, and the invention of damning hypotheses were resorted to in building up the case against the accused. In addition, the jury was allegedly influenced through the unscrupulous use of oratory, legal legerdemain, and a negligent defense.

The present Quebec government, argues Mr. Hébert, should either prove that he is lying and take legal action against him, or institute a Royal Commission to investigate the case and, finally, render such justice as is still possible in the circumstances.

Should the government decide to follow the editor's advice, it may well set off fireworks that would be visible all the way to Vancouver.

THE MODERATE

Mr. Gérard Pelletier, editor of *La Presse,* a hefty Montreal daily which has the largest circulation of any French-language North-American newspaper, is a good representative of the moderate, non-separatist, and yet critical French Canadian who is still interested in reasoning with English-speaking Canada. As reported in *La Presse* of November 15, 1963, he and Mr. Pierre-Elliot Trudeau, whose anti-separatist views have already been summarized, braved a largely separatist gathering of some five hundred University of Montreal students to debate the issue with separatist leaders André d'Allemagne and Pierre Bourgault.

While the separatists argued that Quebec could be no more than a "reserve" in Confederation, their opponents took them to task for spending all their energies to advance their cause and neglecting the "true problems". Mr. Pelletier especially deplored the young people's lack of concern for the working classes, while Mr. Trudeau emphasized the importance of dealing with health, education, urban planning, delinquency, the civil service, and unemployment. (The two men appear to have roughly similar views on separatism). During the debate in question, Trudeau also drew noisy protests from the students by affirming that Ottawa had made better use of tax revenues than had Quebec.

In his March 16 speech to the Vancouver Institute, Pelletier performed, among others, the service of demolishing at least one manifestly false explanation for separatism. Apparently a political scientist at the University of Alberta had explained that "Quebec's separatists hold to their fantastic views on Canadian politics for just one reason: because they remember their French origins. But let them move to the cities . . . let them modernize their thoughts and visit Toronto and they will forget their French origins altogether with their separatist ideas."

Move to the cities! This from a professor about a province whose population is already three-fourths urban, about a province in which two out of every five persons live in Greater Montreal, a city which, is after all, Canada's largest. And Toronto! No one who has lived here for a month could have failed to notice that, in Gérard Pelletier's words "the most excited among them (the separatists) are those who did live in Toronto or Ottawa for a while and were infuriated by the attitudes of some English Canadians towards French culture in Canada and the world."

After demonstrating that separatism isn't associated with the kind of person who could be expected to spend several hours a day in his rocking chair, dreaming of the lost glories of the Sun King, Mr. Pelletier gets down to its "essence".

"The essence of separatism is exactly the same principle which inspires nationalism. Quebec separatists founded their belief on the impossibility for French Canada to develop its culture within the framework of Confederation. They hold that the State of Quebec should be politically independent because the French Canadians are a nation by themselves, because they need an independent political entity as a basis for their culture. What difference is there between this position and that of many English Canadians who believe that Canada should be strictly English speaking and consider the existence of French Canada a nuisance?

"I can say for sure that separatism in Quebec is nothing but a marginal movement, with a tiny membership and a rare talent for making loud noises all over the place." (It is worth noting, however, that nine months later, the speaker met the representatives of this "marginal movement" on equal terms.) "But I am not so sure that English-speaking separatists, that is people who believe that Canada should be an English-speaking country, are not much more numerous. . . . In French Canada we know very well that separatism is a limited phenomenon with very limited importance by itself. . . . I could . . . compare it to the tiny communist parties in Britain, Switzerland or Belgium. They do not mean much as a political force but they are a good barometer of social discontent in these countries. . . . And people who cry shame and separatism as soon as French Canada claims its rights or suggests that Confederation should be revised remind me of the McCarthyists who used to put the communist label on all social claims, including the protest against segregation in the South.

"What the majority of French Canadians want is nothing but the bicultural state envisaged by the Fathers of Confederation, a modern commonwealth free from the prejudices of XIXth century nationalism, a political entity in which both cultural groups would be on an equal footing working side by side for the development of Canada, each in its own way but with common objectives.

"What we want to learn from English Canada is whether English Canadians have changed their minds or not on this basic objective. We think there are serious reasons for doubt.

"In theory, of course, very few people in English Canada question the principle of cultural duality, although there is a minority of extremists who do. If, for instance, you want to infuriate French Canada, all you have to do is point out that there are in Canada such a number of cultural minorities that it is impossible to give special treatment to the French one. Thus having erased three and a half centuries of Canadian history in one stroke, it is easy to put French Canada on the same footing with the German, Polish or Ukrainian minorities, ignoring by the same token that French Canadians number five million, which is many times the size of any other cultural minority in Canada."

English Canadians making speeches, asserted the editor, love to wax eloquent on the sublimities of biculturalism, but back down when practical implications, like bilingualism in government or provincial autonomy are brought up.

"When we talk about French Canadian discontent, this is what we mean. . . . We cannot live on principles alone any more.

"If this country is not prepared to pay the cost of cultural duality, for it does cost something, French Canada will soon come to the conclusion that English Canadian extreme nationalists have won the day, in spite of all the oratory that might survive for a long time.

"So the last question and the most crucial one is the following: Is Canada ready to go along with the practical consequences of biculturalism?

"It is still an open question. But for the time being, French Canada's answer is negative. Why? Because of the practical behaviour of the majority. . . ."

What, if anything, is the monstrous majority doing to redeem itself?

IN THE GREAT TRADITION

Earlier this year, the author had the pleasure of attending a meeting of *Les Amis du Devoir* here in Quebec which was presided over by Mr. Laurendeau in company with Mr. Sauriol and Mr. Ryan. While the entire proceeding was extremely interesting, one could not but feel that Mr. Laurendeau's combination of real concern for the ideas of those present and superb ability to form and express his own constituted one of the best conceivable arguments for biculturalism.

A cover article in *Châtelaine* (June 1963), reminds us again that Quebec is not all fanaticism. The magazine discusses Mrs. Thérèse Casgrain, a lady who, over the last forty years or so, has done much to inspire measures that have given the vote, in provincial elections, to Quebec women, and made them eligible for the bar;

improved the working conditions of women teachers and clerks, made family-allowance cheques payable to mothers, and protected children. Wife of the late Liberal Speaker of the House of Commons, Pierre Casgrain, she, herself, has been head of the C.C.F. party in Quebec. Before the last federal election, she was President of the Voice of Women, well known for its humane concerns and for its opposition to war in general and nuclear war in particular.

Mrs. Casgrain must have obtained her objectives through much perseverance, for her defeat as New Democratic candidate in the last federal election marked the ninth such setback she has received in either federal or Quebec elections. This makes her a kind of Canadian Norman Thomas, if the masculine reference be forgiven in the case of so gracious a lady. Apparently she does not depend on revolution, having had the faith, courage, and sanity to pursue her ideals consistently through the years, despite repeated personal frustration. In late years, she has made a number of cross-country speaking tours to explain the French-Canadian context, and to lecture on more universal themes to Canadian audiences. Now, as before, she is deeply involved in broadening the concept of the civil rights of women in Quebec and of Canadians at large. She believes firmly that there are more things that join Canadians together than divide them; that many of the great problems that they face can only be solved together. The calm wisdom of such people tempers the brash impatience of the times. It was André Laurendeau who stated in a *Le Devoir* editorial during her election campaign, that the "best man in Outremont-St. John is Thérèse Casgrain."

THE BALANCE SHEET

Although he feels that his importance is, for now at least, largely eclipsed by his powerful neighbour, the English Canadian recognizes no superiors and few equals when it comes to being democratic and to judging every man on his merits, with no distinctions based on race, language, religion, origin, or anything like that. From the virgin snows of his True North Strong and Free (free except for American economic domination, he grumbles), away up at the top of the map, he looks down with infinite disdain upon the renegades of South Africa and the drawling white Lotus Eaters of the Land of Cotton. Paralyzed (as he sees it) by perpetual sun and too-easy living, these lesser mortals of less rigorous climes are far too idle to do anything about the vast compost heaps of rot and decay that overwhelm them on all sides; in their degenerate state, they can but expend what little strength is left to them in brewing up evil-smelling cauldrons of racial magic, the sole purpose of which is to shift the blame for the whole hopeless mess onto somebody else.

Holding such views, English Canadians must receive with some shock and surprise French Canada's accusations of unfairness and prejudice. They have, however, made some attempts to better matters, attempts which have received considerable notice and attention in French-speaking Quebec.

To begin with, there have been a number of initiatives to increase the teaching of French throughout the land. Quebec City's *Soleil* comments favourably, in an editorial of July 6, 1963, as follows:

"It is more and more evident that the cause of French in Canada has for some time been advancing in many provinces of Canada. A few weeks ago, Charlottetown put the teaching of French on its primary school program. Last week, Manitoba decided on the importance of teaching French in the elementary schools beginning in 1963, when it will be taught in the first year. . . .

"The tendency to teach a second language thus shows signs of becoming generalized throughout the country. The day may not be far off when all the provinces will agree and will take the necessary measures in this sense. The position of bilingualism will be much stronger. English as the second language in Quebec, French as the second language in the English provinces, there is what could make Canadian unity an emphatic reality, full of promise."

Le Devoir of September 20 reports that the theory put forth by famous brain surgeon Dr. Wilder Penfield, to the effect that the younger one begins to learn a second language the better, is gaining ever-increasing acceptance in Canadian schools.

Six out of ten provinces, says *Le Devoir*, have more complete French courses, both in the primary and secondary schools, than ever before.

Manitoba is given credit for offering French to French Canadians in Grade One.

Edmonton's new policy of teaching French in Grades Four to Six, at least in schools that are close to high-schools where French is taught, receives recognition.

In Regina, we read, ten Catholic separate schools are adding French in Grades Seven and Eight.

Vancouver is teaching French in Grades Eight to Ten.

In Ontario, more and more primary schools have French.

Montreal is starting, experimentally, the teaching of French in Grade One — in its English Protestant schools.

A number of private schools like St. George's, The Study and Weston School in Westmount, have been teaching French from Kindergarten up, for years. They use only teachers whose native language is French.

On November 14, *Le Soleil* once again accords editorial recognition to the goodwill shown by the six provinces that teach French at both levels, although it has reservations about many of the teachers since their knowledge of French is purely theoretical.

The reader will recall Mr. Jean-Charles Harvey's view that separatism would quickly disappear if the preponderantly English provinces would stop anglicizing in the schools.

Privy Council President Maurice Lamontagne has been taking measures to realize bilingualism in the federal government. Exams for civil-service candidates are being changed to give French-Canadians a better chance. Special courses in French are to be given to a number of civil servants who are already on the job. A bilingual Civil Service Institute is planned, and candidates for a diplomatic career will henceforth have to write exams in both French and English.

At this writing, the Canadian Council of Resources Ministers has met for the second time in Montreal (the first meeting took place a year ago in Toronto). The *Montreal Star* of November 15 describes it as the first permanent government body in Canada founded on the principle of equality between the eleven senior governments, for here the federal minister sits as an equal with all the others, as is not the case in the usual federal-provincial conference. Designed to organize cooperation between the provinces in the use of their natural resources without domination by Ottawa, the Council, very appropriately, had the Honourable René Lévesque as its president this year.

Among Crown Corporations, there have been a number of measures designed to give more satisfaction to French-speaking Canadians. Beginning in January, 1964, Trans-Canada Airlines (*Air Canada* in French) is to give French courses to English flight personnel in Montreal. It is announced that Montreal is to be a bilingual airport by 1965 — that is, all officers and hostesses on flights leaving Montreal will speak both the official languages. In addition, after May 1, 1964, all TCA personnel serving in Europe are to be bilingual.

Has ever an English-Canadian gone from a state of opprobrium in French-Canadian minds to acceptance or near-acceptance as brilliantly as has CN president Mr. Donald Gordon? After the disturbances of November 1962, Mr. Gordon became very silent and managed to stay out of the headlines until September 1963. It will be recalled that his mandate as CN chief expired at the end of September, a fact which, in view of his extreme unpopularity in Quebec and his considerable unpopularity in English Canada, seemed to make it very likely that his $75,000.00 a year job, the highest paid in Canadian government, was about to go to someone else. But Mr. Gordon was, everyone conceded, an excellent administrator, and he was about to show this in a surprising way.

Mr. Gordon unfair to French Canadian? Why (he said) just look at the record!

Since the beginning of 1963, forty-five per cent of CN's French Canadian 'senior officers' had been promoted or moved to a position giving them greater opportunity for advancement.

A program of recruiting French-Canadian graduates and undergraduates, begun previously, had been accelerated since November of 1962, doubling the number of French Canadians so hired in 1963.

A program favouring the promotion of French Canadians had been put into effect.

A French and English language instruction program had been started for CN volunteers who need to be more bilingual for their jobs or whose normal opportunities for promotion could be hindered by failure to know both languages.

Plans had also been made to increase the railway's bilingual publications, forms, posters, menus, advertising, station signs, headquarters' building signs, office identifications, etc.

The author's interview with Mr. René Lévesque in connection with the CBC strike of 1959 shows that even such action as this does not immediately allay all fears and suspicions of all French Canadians. On the other hand, there can be no doubt that Mr. Gordon's good-will campaign met with considerable success.

"By choosing to act rather than to speak too much, Mr. Gordon has shown that his remarks of November 1962 applied specifically to the view that a man should be hired merely because of his faith, his race, or his language," writes Claude Ryan in an October 7 editorial in *Le Devoir*.

The Government offered to reappoint Mr. Gordon to his position. Mr. Gordon replied that although he would like to be relieved of his responsibilities, he wished to complete certain projects which, he said, should take about a year and a half. He would then ask to be relieved of his duties.

So far in this section we have looked at current developments that appear likely to improve French-English relations and Canada's chances of survival as a single great country. Working in the opposite sense, we have a recent speech by Premier Bennett of British Columbia. His major assertions were that B.C. won't stand for any basic changes in Confederation, that B.C. makes "fiscal sacrifices" for Confederation, that "subsidies" by B.C. and Ontario to Quebec totalled sixty-four million dollars last year. Mr. Bennett does not believe that bilingualism should be required of B.C.'s federal civil servants or that federal civil servants should be given a bonus for bilingualism.

December, 1963. The separatists, the pure separatists, like Pierre Bourgeault, Marcel Chaput, Raymond Barbeau, and André d'Allemagne are still with us. It must be said that they have never succeeded in monopolizing all headlines in the way that they apparently desire.

Dr. Chaput's hunger strike this summer (he refused to eat until his party received $100,000) did, after more than a month, bring in the desired amount. It is very doubtful, though, whether it increased the separatist's prestige and influence, and it may even have had the opposite effect. Recently, he was on another hunger strike for fifty thousand dollars, which does not appear to have been very successful either.

The Government of Quebec itself, with its demands for increased autonomy and powers of taxation, has advanced and is advancing so rapidly that its declarations and demands tend to overshadow those of the original separatists. The Federal-Provincial Conference, which began on November 25, and ended inconclusively just in time for the Grey Cup game, was described by Municipal Affairs Minister Pierre Laporte as "the beginning of the major task of remaking the Constitution of 1867. . . . we might have to resign ourselves to leaving Confederation if Quebec is not given more autonomy" (*Le Devoir*, November 11).

Thus we see that at this point separatism is an option that is officially accepted. Given the ever-increasing pressures and speed of the revolution, Quebec could be officially separatist long before we celebrate the Centenary of Confederation in 1967. It seems that

Canada can be saved, but not without real effort on the part of a good many Canadians, here in Quebec and elsewhere.

We have, of course, the Royal Commission on Biculturalism, with co-chairmen Mr. Dunton and Mr. Laurendeau. Readers of these pages will have seen what a severe, penetrating critic of English Canada Mr. Laurendeau can be. Yet notwithstanding all the faults he finds in his country, one senses throughout all his work a genuine, sincere struggle to understand as well as to be understood. While others who do not have Mr. Laurendeau's record as a French-Canadian nationalist simply follow the general drift towards nationalism and separatism, Mr. Laurendeau, in spite of all temptations, really has made his choice in favour of Canada as well as of Quebec, and though he may be a man difficult to win, he is much to be depended upon. Though he is part of the revolution this book deals with and, as shown in its pages (the author hopes not unfairly), at times scarcely distinguishable in his ideas from many others who are swept up by it, he yet retains a certain individuality, a certain separateness, that tends rather to increase than diminish with the passage of time. He yet testifies to the fact that the human spirit is greater than the circumstances in which it finds itself.

As we conclude this short survey of some of the more striking aspects of contemporary Quebec life, it is not superfluous to recall that at the heart of the revolution is not the relations of Quebec with Canada as a whole, important as these are, but the internal relations of French-speaking Quebecer with French-speaking Quebecer. At the heart of it is Brother Anonymous, not physically present perhaps, but present in a book and present in his ideas. It is his passionate concern for Quebec's whole philosophy and way of life that lies behind the headlines of our daily papers.

APPENDIX

DONALD GORDON'S DAY
IN COURT

The dialogue between CN President Donald Gordon and his critics shows what can happen when French and English Canadians get down to cases. Clearly, both sides are likely to receive some rude shocks when they talk business about biculturalism. Nevertheless, if there can be a true desire to show patience and understanding on both sides, and there must be this if we are to have anything more constructive than bombs, then we might almost wish for a great many frank, no-holds-barred discussions like those recorded in this appendix. At this stage it would do English and French Canadians very little good to create, say, the Tea-Sippers' Mutual Congratulation Society, or something of the kind. Mr. Gordon and his questioners may symbolize for us the difficulties we will have to face, as well as the opportunities for progress that may offer themselves, when we think of making biculturalism something more than a pale, philosophical abstraction.

Accordingly we present, unabridged, that part of the official minutes of the Sessional Committee on Railways, Air Lines and Shipping (November, 1962) which appears to have touched off the storm of protest against Mr. Gordon's alleged unfairness to French Canadians, which made all the headlines. Answering the charges against him, Mr. Gordon gave an interview to the Montreal newspaper *La Presse* which we also reproduce here.

MINUTES OF THE SESSIONAL COMMITTEE ON
RAILWAYS, AIR LINES AND SHIPPING,
NOVEMBER, 1962*

Mr. Grégoire: I had another point I wanted to mention, and it is in connection with the first page of the report. I note we have one president, seventeen vice-presidents and ten directors, and none of them is French Canadian.

Mr. Gordon: How do you know?

* Pages 59-66.

Mr. Grégoire: Then, which ones are?

Mr. Gordon: I want to find out from you who is French Canadian.

Mr. Grégoire: Could you name for me the ones who are.

Mr. Gordon: I do not know how to define a French Canadian. But I will say this: these are all Canadians, every one of them.

Mr. Grégoire: They are not names of French speaking Canadians.

Mr. Gordon: There are some French speaking Canadians on the board of directors.

Mr. Foy: Mr. J. Louis Levesque is on the board of directors.

Mr. Gordon: There are several members who can speak French, if that is what you want to know.

Mr. Grégoire: We do not wish to impose upon you and have all French speaking Canadians on the board of directors but we feel entitled to have some French speaking Canadians named thereto.

Mr. Gordon: Let me say quite clearly that the promotion policy of the Canadian National Railways has always been based upon promotion by merit. The man who, by reason of experience, knowledge, judgment, education or for any other reason, is considered by the management to be the best person fitted for a job will receive the promotion, and we do not care whether he is black, white, red or French. Even Scotsmen receive promotion in the C.N.R. We never ask questions of that kind in regard to promotion or employment, and I think if we did we would be following a practice against the Canadian Fair Employment Practices Act which, by law, tells us that we must not discriminate because of race, national origin, colour, religion or age.

Mr. Grégoire: Mr. Gordon, you perhaps do not wish to take language into consideration, but if some consideration were given in this regard perhaps we would not see the situation develop in Quebec which we now see there on occasion, with the result that on lines between Montreal and Chicoutimi or Montreal and Quebec individuals riding on the train cannot understand what the trainmen say.

I should like to ask you another question. Were you not able to find any French speaking Canadians qualified to be named to the board of directors as listed on the first page of the annual report?

Mr. Gordon: That is not a correct statement.

The Chairman: Mr. Guy Charbonneau and Mr. J. Louis Levesque are named on that list of board of directors.

Mr. Grégoire: Yes, but board of directors in French would be "direction" or "selection".

Mr. Gordon: I repeat that we do not attempt in C.N.R. practice to break down types of Canadians. Our employment opportunities are open to all Canadians, and our promotional policy is based on the fact that promotions are made regardless, as I quoted the Canadian Fair Employment Practices Act, of race, national origin, colour, religion or age. That requirement is set out in an act of this country. It is part of the law of this land and we carry it out.

Mr. Grégoire: Does it follow from what you have said that there were no French speaking Canadians qualified to hold these positions or there were no French speaking Canadians who made application for these positions?

Mr. Gordon: We have officers and employees who are able to speak French in all positions where there is such a requirement in order to serve the public. I think our record in that respect is better than most organizations in this country.

In regard to making promotions of any kind in this group that you have referred to, there are men who speak French. You cannot judge by name whether a man speaks French or otherwise. I am aware of a number of names of French speaking Canadians which do not appear to me to be French names at all.

Mr. Fisher: A good example of that is the name "O'Hurley".

Mr. Gordon: Perhaps the name "Fisher" is a French name for all I know.

The Chairman: Even the minister can speak French.

Mr. Grégoire: Could you give us some detail concerning those individuals named on this list of board of directors who are bilingual?

Mr. Gordon: You are referring to them being bilingual in what respect?

Mr. Chevrier: Mr. Chairman, I fully agree with what Mr. Grégoire has said as one looks at this page. I say with all due respect to the president of the C.N.R. and I have known him for a long time, he is not prejudiced in the slightest degree. Having said that, I think it is a misnomer to put an annual report before the parliament of Canada including this list of names indicating that you have not been able to find one qualified individual in the province of Quebec. That situation is not understandable. It is all right to say that there are no discriminatory practices and so forth and so on, but an organization such as the Canadian National Railways ought to be able to find people who are able to fulfill these positions, and who are French speaking. You have had no difficulty in this regard in respect of the board of directors, one of whom is J. Louis Levesque, one of the most outstanding French Canadian businessmen in Canada. You apparently had no difficulty in naming him to the board of directors, and I cannot commend management enough for that appointment, but surely similar appointments are possible in other fields.

Mr. Gordon: Mr. Chevrier, may I say this? We are speaking of a group of men as listed here, all of whom have arrived at these positions on the railways, if you are referring to railway men, as the result of 20 or 30 years' experience. This may be the result of a policy of 20 or 30 years ago which produced these men but not a policy for which I am responsible today. We have done more for the cause of the French language in the C.N.R. than any other organization in Canada.

Mr. Chevrier: You cannot make me believe that in an organization such as the Canadian National Railways there are no men of the standing and level of those who are listed on the second page of the annual report who are French speaking who could fill these positions. I do not want to be unfair or unjust, but it seems to me a misnomer for an organization such as the C.N.R. to say that there are no French speaking Canadians of that calibre. I do not believe such a statement.

Mr. Gordon: Mr. Chevrier, let me say this. What you really are asking for is discrimination.

Mr. Chevrier: I am not asking for discrimination at all.

Mr. Gordon: Yes, you are.

Mr. Chevrier: It may be that I could give you names, Mr. Gordon, but I will not give them publicly, who fit this category.

Mr. Gordon: I would be glad to have them, I assure you.

Mr. Chevrier: Just a moment, I will give you these names afterwards, names of people who, in my opinion and in the opinion of many people in the province of Quebec, should have obtained promotion because of their knowledge and because of their experience in the C.N.R., but who were not given promotions.

Mr. Gordon: I can assure you of this, and I want to make this statement clear. In respect of these promotions, and particularly during our recent reorganization, there was not one of these appointments made before we had combed every possible analysis that we could devise to make certain that the man who got the position was the best qualified. There was no discrimination in that respect. The fact that you do not recognize a French speaking Canadian's name in that group has nothing whatever to do with the choice. I deny emphatically on behalf of management that there has been any discrimination in this regard and say to you that we have a completely non-discriminatory policy, and that we have chosen the men who were qualified.

Mr. Chevrier: I accept your denial but say that for nine years I have heard the same explanation that you are giving this committee now by your predecessor and by others. However, I repeat what I said earlier, that in so far as you personally are concerned there is not the slightest prejudice involved. I know that to be true, but there is something wrong some place. I only ask those of you in connection with this who are operating the railway to give this matter a little more serious consideration.

Mr. Gordon: We cannot give it more serious consideration than we have given it.

Mr. Chevrier: You will not do anything about it then?

Mr. Gordon: I can give you part of the reason for the difficulty that you have referred to. I could give you chapter and verse, but I will ask you to accept my word for this, in respect of French speaking Canadians who could have filled certain positions but who refused to accept promotion because they did not want to leave the province of Quebec, or because they did not want to leave the city of Quebec or Montreal, as the case may be. If we are going to educate our officers and make them qualified they must be willing to go anywhere in Canada in the course of their training. This situation gives rise to one stumbling block.

I could give you chapter and verse of a French speaking Canadian, a gentleman that you know very well, who I was on the verge of appointing as vice-president, but who went to what he thought was a better job in the province of Quebec.

Another difficulty involved is that these French speaking Canadians who are qualified are under premium demand today.

Mr. Chevrier: I will be glad to discuss that particular case with you at any time.

Mr. Gordon: I could give you the man's name.

Mr. Chevrier: I know the name and I am very familiar with the circumstances, but they are not as clear as you have stated.

Mr. Gordon: Let me say this to you. I will stick my neck out this far; when I come back here ten years from now you will find that some of the men we have employed in the last two or three years will be occupying some of the positions to which you refer. We have recruited a great number of French speaking Canadians from universities, for example, in an effort to solve this problem. We have employed many individuals in this category, and this policy is working very well. It will be some time before we see the results of this policy, but in a few years I am sure you will see a change. That is why I say to you when you ask me to give serious consideration to this, and I hope you will accept my word, that it has had most serious consideration.

Mr. Pugh: Mr. Gordon, you said in answer to questions in this regard, "We—" and I should like to know whether you mean by that the board of directors?

Mr. Gordon: I had reference to the management of the C.N.R. which includes the board of directors, yes.

Mr. Pugh: In regard to this discussion I note that you have listed on the board of directors Mr. Levesque and Mr. Charbonneau.

Mr. Balcer: Mr. Ayers is French speaking also.

Mr. Gordon: A lot of these promotions are made on my personal recommendation. They come up to me from the regional officers, and they come through to me as chief executive officer of the railways. I bring them before the board of directors and they hear all there is to be said about it.

Mr. Pugh: On all senior appointments?

Mr. Gordon: Yes.

Mr. Rouleau: You mean to say that in your own judgment there are no French speaking Canadians with the proper qualities and the capacity to become officers of the company? You have not been able to find French speaking Canadians in the province of Quebec who in your own judgment would have the capacity to be appointed as officers in a country like ours?

Mr. Grégoire: How can you explain that, when we have a Minister of Transport who is a French speaking Canadian, you cannot find other French speaking Canadians having enough merit to be members on the board of directors of the Canadian National Railways?

Mr. Gordon: Both of you are distorting what I have said. I am saying that we are not discriminating in connection with our promotions. Of course, we have a number of senior officers, for example the general manager of the St. Lawrence region whom you could call a French Canadian, and in terms of selecting these particular positions to be filled when they become vacant, for example, this man who was appointed had a better entitlement to the job in terms of ability, qualifications and experience which goes into making a judgment. Everyone on the railway who had a right to be considered for that job was duly considered and eventually we made a choice. However, we did not make a choice because the man was an English speaking Canadian or a French speaking Canadian or anything else, only that he was a Canadian. Each one of these men was selected as being best qualified at the particular time the appointment was made. I do not want to say for a moment that we have not able French Canadians in our service, particularly in the province of Quebec—of course we have.

Mr. Grégoire: But not enough to find one, or a couple of them or six, to put on the board of directors?

Mr. Gordon: Let me say this—perhaps I was speaking indiscreetly, I manage to talk myself into an indiscretion now and again — as far as I am personally concerned and as long as I am president of the C.N.R., there is not going to be a promotion or an appointment made just because a man is a French Canadian. He has got to be a French Canadian plus other things, and he has to be as able as the other fellow who has a claim on the job. There is going to be fair practice on the C.N.R. as long as I am there. What you are arguing for is discrimination.

Mr. Grégoire: Do you intend to say there are no able French Canadians in the province of Quebec, who are as able as the officers you have appointed?

Mr. Gordon: That is a distortion of what I said. When one of these jobs become vacant, if any of them dropped dead tomorrow — which God forbid — when the management sits down to consider it, anyone in the railways who has the qualifications, experience, education or anything else, will be considered for it. If he happens to be what you call a French Canadian, he will get it.

Mr. Grégoire: But you were not able to find anyone in the past years.

Mr. Gordon: At the time these appointments were made, I repeat, the best man was chosen.

Mr. Rouleau: Would it not be possible to make a special effort to find a qualified French speaking Canadian for the job?

Mr. Gordon: You are asking me to discriminate.

Mr. Rouleau: It is only fair.

Mr. Grégoire: Mr. Gordon, they were found less able in your judgment, is that right?

Mr. Gordon: Let me say that the man chosen for the job was the best person available at the time.

Mr. Grégoire: In your own judgment?

Mr. Gordon: In the judgment of myself and my advisors and in the judgment of the people who worked with him and who made the recommendations. I do not run a one-man show. By the time we make that appointment I have probably received ten or twelve different appraisals. We have a staff folder giving the man's record. All these things are examined over the years to see where the man fits best.

Mr. Grégoire: Was the judgment that led you to find those people more able than any French speaking Canadian the same as the one you used to name the C.N.R. hotel which we all know of despite the protestations of all the people in Montreal?

Mr. Fisher: I think these questions are not to the point. Maybe Mr. Gordon could tell us what are the inhibiting factors at the present time that seem to keep the people who might be called French Canadian — I do not know how you define that — away from these positions? Mr. Gordon has mentioned the past, but I would like to know the facts. Is it because the C.N.R. conducts all its business in English?

Mr. Gordon: I do not think so. We do not conduct all our business in English. Our train operating rules are written in English for the simple reason that there can only be one language when you are dealing with issuing such rules, just as it is in the army. If you are issuing orders, you must have one language which everybody realizes means the same thing or you will get into dangerous difficulties on the question of interpretation. There can be no question about that. But if you ask me to make a general statement, I will say this, that the C.N.R. — or indeed the railways of Canada — have not apparently been regarded as an employment field where we have been able to attract the brighter men of French Canada, and we have not had the men. Over the past ten years we have gone at this thing very definitely. I started it myself, and I can claim credit for it — although I am sure I will not get it — that we started examining right away to see how we could improve the content, so to speak, of our staff to get French Canadians with ability and education. As a result of this, for instance, in 1961 — Mr. Vaughan just called my attention to it — out of 42 university graduates whom we took on our staff from all across Canada, there were 11 who were from Laval or Montreal university. That is 25 per cent. We got those by going after them. In due course those men will feed in other people from French Canada, if we do not lose them. I found from experience — and I would point this out to Mr. Chevrier in particular — that when we do find a French Canadian and we develop him and he begins to stick his head up and begins to be recognized, we lose him.

Mr. Fisher: What about the prospect of bringing French Canadians in who have experience outside, bringing them in on an executive level in your organization?

Mr. Gordon: We would do that if there was a need for it, but I do not think it is fair to prejudice the existing employees in the C.N.R. who have made it their life's work by bringing in men over their heads if we do not need them. We have however brought some in.

Mr. Chevrier: You have done that in one or two cases.

Mr. Fisher: Because of special circumstances and whenever these special circumstances may obtain, they will get special consideration.

Mr. Grégoire: What was your experience with the C.N.R. before you were nominated as president?

Mr. Gordon: I never worked in the C.N.R.

Mr. Grégoire: When you came to the C.N.R. was it in prejudice to the people there?

Mr. Gordon: That would have to be answered by the people who appointed me.

Mr. Grégoire: You have said something about the rules of the C.N.R. being in English so as to avoid misunderstanding. Do you mean that the laws of the government of Canada, which are in both languages, can bring about misunderstanding between Canadian citizens and the judges.

Mr. Gordon: I would not want to comment on that. I am not enough in the courts. But it seems to me there is plenty of confusion in the laws of Canada. When you give an order to a man, whether it be in the army or the railway, that order must be precise, and mean one thing. We only know there is no time to translate when there is danger.

Mr. Grégoire: Do you think there would be danger in translating the rules of the Canadian National Railways?

Mr. Gordon: Yes, very definitely.

Mr. Grégoire: Do you think it would be more dangerous than to translate the laws of the government of Canada?

Mr. Gordon: Yes, very definitely, and quite obviously, because there are differences in translation. You have asked me for an opinion, while you give your own.

Mr. Fisher: I would like Mr. Gordon to have an opportunity to answer the question.

Mr. Gordon: Let me illustrate it by giving you a little story covering my own initial experience with bilingualism. Before I entered the railway, I was in the Bank of Canada, and we found it necessary to demolish an old building in order to build the Bank of Canada. In my innocence, I awarded the tender to the lowest tenderer, who happened to be a French-speaking contractor, named Lajeunesse. I do not know if he is yet around. But there was a terrible row in the city of Ottawa. Why would we give the contract to a French speaking contractor when there were plenty of English speaking ones here?

I called the contractor in and said to him: Surely it ought to be possible to employ some men who are English speaking Canadians? Why do you have to take all French speaking Canadians, mostly from Hull, to do the job?"

The contractor said: "This is dangerous work."

I said, "surely you can get English speaking Canadians to do dangerous work?"

He said: "That is not the point, that building is 5 or 6 stories high, and there is a big steel beam up there. Let us say there are two employees on it, and that beam is about to fall. The foreman yells 'jump!' There is no time to translate." It is exactly the same thing with the railway.

Mr. Grégoire: Do you often have to jump out of your trains?

The Chairman: He might have to. It seems to me that we are on the first page of the report.

Mr. Grégoire: On a question of privilege, the rules of the Canadian National Railways are all in English.

Mr. Gordon: I am not talking about the rules generally for employees. Certainly we publish our general rules in English and in French. We have page after page of them. I am talking about the train operating rules, the running rules which cover the movement of trains, the physical movement of trains, the running orders affecting the movement of trains. That is a very small segment.

There is an authorized operating rule book which is common to all railways in Canada as well as on the North American continent; it is the same with the United States, and it is agreed on between all the railways, so that a certain thing means the same thing on every railway. Those are orders; those are running rules.

The other rules are all our information to staff and everything that we publish, such as our management bulletins, and everything that we put out for the information of staff, and this we send out in French and English. I have a long list of things which we do in this regard.

Mr. Grégoire: I thought we were speaking of the rules of the Canadian National Railways, and that this would have been the reason why French Canadians are not more fully engaged in the administration.

Mr. Gordon: No; it is a different thing altogether.

Mr. Fisher: We have had it expressed here in the way of some fairly strong opinions that it would be advantageous in many ways if we did have some French Canadians in executive positions with the Canadian National Railways. If I understood your reply, your policy is that you will not discriminate either for or against, and that your appointments are made on the basis of merit and ability.

Mr. Gordon: That is right.

Mr. Fisher: Assuming that that is a fair policy and that you are continuing it, you are still seeking to bring into your executive force people with French Canadian Background.

Mr. Gordon: We are looking for them and are anxious to get them.

Mr. Rideout: I hope that when Mr. Gordon is choosing people from the universities for future high positions in the railways he will not forget St. Joseph's University.

Mr. Gordon: You can't win!

The following is a translation, published December 12, 1962, of an interview with CN President Donald Gordon conducted by the Montreal newspaper, *La Presse.*

"As I have been away on a trip to the United States, only on my return was I able to review, with some delay, the comment published last week in Canadian newspapers. I was most concerned to learn that, despite my assurances to the contrary, some sections of public opinion continue to insist that Canadian National practices discrimination against French Canadians in matters of promotions and appointments."

Those words were spoken by Donald Gordon, President of the Canadian National Railways, a man who has been hanged in effigy by students in several cities, the most controversial figure in Canada since his recent appearance before a committee of the House of Commons.

Mr. Gordon had kept until now, amid the storm, the most complete silence. *La Presse* had been wondering if he had any comment to make. A phone call revealed that he had. This is how we found ourselves in the presence of this tall strapping man, ageing but sturdy, blinking behind thick glasses, who expresses his thoughts with great precision.

La Presse: In all the comment, what is it that impressed you most?

Mr. Gordon: The remarks of Mr. Jean Marchand, Chairman of the Confederation of National Trade Unions. He has stated that "discrimination exists not at the moment when a man is named to an important office, but further back, when the system begins to groom potential executives". This is criticism that I would be willing to explore with Mr. Marchand, in an effort to ascertain the facts.

La Presse: Is this criticism serious, in your opinion?

Mr. Gordon: It will be obvious to anyone that I cannot be expected personally to know all the circumstances surrounding each and every transfer, promotion and appointment in an organization which employs more than one hundred thousand people. I can only say that the *policy* of management, in these matters, is that promotions be granted, whenever possible, to men who are already in the service of Canadian National and that the best qualified men be chosen. Mr. Marchand seems to think however, that this system is faulty and has resulted in discriminatory practices of which I am not aware. If this should be so, it is my duty to discover such practices. I would be happy to discuss the matter personally with Mr. Marchand, a responsible labour leader whose opinions I respect. If the system to which Mr. Marchand refers can be improved so as better to ensure fair and equitable treatment, I would be the first to recommend that the necessary changes be made.

La Presse: Does that mean, Mr. Gordon, that you favour a private investigation in order to avoid the public investigation that has been requested from the Government by our newspaper and several others?

Mr. Gordon: Not in the least. On the contrary, I believe that the best solution would be to create a royal commission that would be given the task of examining the whole matter of Canada as a bicultural country and the consequences of that fact. And not only at the CN, but everywhere: in the civil service, the major industrial companies and all public utility organizations. Far from having any objection to such an investigation, I consider it as the great means of attaining factual, scientific knowledge of the problems involved and of developing satisfactory solutions.

The conversation suddenly takes a new turn. Until now, the newspaperman has abstained from referring to the past statements of Mr. Gordon. He had been waiting for the latter to lead the way back into the past:

La Presse: So, you believe in the bi-ethnical character of Canada?

Mr. Gordon: It is a fact.

La Presse: Your testimony before the railway committee gave the impression that you did not recognize this fact.

Mr. Gordon: But I also did not recognize, on reading newspaper accounts, the testimony that I had given. I was even quoted as saying: "I shall never employ French Canadians anymore." Those are words that I have never said.

La Presse: I am neither referring to newspaper accounts nor to televised comment, but to the official transcript of your testimony. In answer to a member of Parliament who was questioning you, you said: "I do not know how to define a French Canadian. But I will say this: these (the vice-presidents of CN) are all Canadians."

And further on, you stated: "There are several members of the board of directors who can speak French, if that is what you want to know." To any French Canadian listener, these two sentences amount to denying the very existence of French Canada and of the bicultural character of Canada.

Mr. Gordon: I am willing to admit that these answers are unfortunate if they create the impression that you mention.

La Presse: But why did you give them?

Mr. Gordon: Do you know the atmosphere in which these committee sittings are held? A question is thrown at you suddenly. You do not expect it and you are required to answer immediately. If I have produced the impression that I think there are no French-Canadians, I certainly did not mean it.

La Presse: But further, when another M.P. insisted on the fact that not one of the vice-presidents of the CN was a French Canadian, you replied: "Allow me to say this: what you are asking of me is to practise discrimination." You do not see any discrimination in the absolute absence of French Canadians but the idea of appointing some appears to you as discrimination?

Mr. Gordon: I am opposed to two ideas, namely that of appointing French Canadians without regard for competence and solely because they are of French culture, and the idea of creating a system of "quotas".

La Presse: French Canadians are the first to second you on the first point; they have never asked to be favoured by being appointed to positions for which they do not fill the requirements. But they maintain that in a democracy, those who pay must be represented at the time the expenditures are made. Consequently, they think that a service such as the CN, which is financed with public monies, should care for a fair representation of the two main cultural groups of Canada, at the level of management as well as at that of manpower. You, Mr. Gordon, give an impression of complete indifference in this matter, one would think that you even refuse to consider the problem.

Mr. Gordon: I could easily show that such an impression is false. When we began, nine years ago, to enter into relations with the universities in view of attracting graduates to the CN, we took exactly the same steps with the French language universities as we did with those of the English language.

La Presse: Do you admit that care for the recruiting and promoting of able men must be accompanied with care for a fair representation for French Canadians?

Mr. Gordon: Not only do I admit it, but it is applied at the CN. I could tell you of many instances: our training courses, grants for extension studies, etc.

La Presse: How do you explain, then, the poor results that are obtained? Not one single French Canadian vice-president, only 13% of the personnel (refers to upper-middle and senior management) etc.?

Mr. Gordon: I shall never claim that we are perfect and I am willing to admit that we have not always done what we could have done. But there are several causes for that:

a) The legacy of the past. It is not for me to call my predecessors to account, but as a matter of fact I have only been responsible since 1949.

b) The fact that French Canadians have not always shown the same interest as today for technical and management callings. I know that this fact is consistently being drummed into your ears, but it has something to do with the present situation.

c) The fact that since the war, the railways have not proved as attractive as they once were. Many promising French Canadians have left us in favour of more interesting fields in industry and commerce.

d) The railway industry is international by nature. The language spoken there, at the higher management levels, due to the necessity of contacts with foreign countries, is the English language.

e) The need for a railway system such as ours to effect transfers in personnel. It is a fact that French Canadians do not like to move away.

f) Lastly, and we may be reminded here of Mr. Marchand's remarks, there is no denying that men in positions of authority like to be surrounded by the people they know best, who speak the same language, share the same culture. Does this factor play an important part? Does it give rise to discrimination? This would require close study.

Do not misunderstand me. I believe that none of the factors I have just mentioned can explain fully a situation that we find deplorable. I say only that each of them carries its influence. Through a serious investigation, it would be possible to measure the relative importance of each one.

Before leaving Mr. Gordon, we asked him, point-blank, a last question:

La Presse: You do not intend to resign?

Mr. Gordon: Do you think that such a move on my part would solve the problem we have just discussed?

La Presse: No. Most French-Canadian newspapers, including ours, have pointed out to their readers that the objective is not to overthrow you, but to get an investigation and efficient action.

Mr. Gordon: For my part, I do not like to resign at the moment when I am attacked.

FOOTNOTES

CHAPTER TWO

1. Herbert F. Quinn, *The Union Nationale* (University of Toronto Press, 1963), p. 95.
2. Ibid. 95-96
3. Ibid. 96
4. Ibid. 158-159-160
5. Marcel Chaput, *Pourquoi je suis séparatiste* (Montréal: Les Editions du Jour, 1961), published in English translation by Ryerson Press, Toronto, 1962, as *Why I Am A Separatist.*
6. Ibid. 132
7. Ibid. 151

CHAPTER THREE

1. Pierre Laporte, *Le vrai visage de Duplessis* (Montreal: Les Editions de l'Homme, 1960), published in translation as *The True Face of Duplessis* by Harvest House, Montreal, June 1960.
2. Ibid. 19
3. Ibid. 67
4. Ibid 76
5. Ibid. 77
6. Ibid. 34
7. Ibid. 46
8. Ibid. 27
9. Ibid. 28
10. Ibid. 63
11. Ibid. 75, 76
12. Ibid. 22
13. *The Impertinences of Brother Anonymous* (Montreal: Harvest House, 1962), p. 57.
14. Abbés Gérard Dion et Louis O'Neill, *Le Chrétien et les élections* (Montréal: Les Editions de l'Homme, 1960).
15. Ibid. 9

16. Ibid. 114, 118, 121
17. *Les insolences du Frère Untel.*
18. Ibid. 71
19. Ibid. 27
20. Ibid. 27, 28
21. Ibid. 29
22. Ibid. 30
23. Ibid. 30
24. Ibid. 47
25. Ibid. 49
26. Ibid. 59
27. Ibid. 61
28. Ibid. 68, 69
29. Ibid. 36

CHAPTER FOUR

1. *Le magazine Maclean* (Montréal: Les Editions Maclean-Hunter Ltée, mars 1961).
2. Ibid. 3
3. Ibid. 19
4. Ibid. 26
5. *Pourquoi je suis séparatiste,* p. 15.
6. Ibid. 31
7. Ibid. 32
8. Ibid. 32
9. Ibid. 34
10. Ibid. 78
11. Ibid. 145
12. Ibid. 68
13. Ibid. 17. The "six dimensions" of separatism are "historical, political, economic, cultural, social and psychological". The numerical problem is one of Dr. Chaput's chief preoccupations.
14. Ibid. 62-64
15. Ibid. 55
16. Ibid. 45
17. Ibid. 135
18. Raymond Barbeau, *J'ai choisi l'indépendance* (Montréal:

Les Editions de l'Homme, 1961).
19. Ibid. 15, 19, 27
20. *Le Canada, expérience ratée ou réussie? (The Canadian Experiment: Success or Failure?)*; (Quebec: Les presses de l'Université Laval, 1962).
21. Ibid. 116
22. Ibid. 155
23. Ibid. 155, 156

CHAPTER FIVE

1. André Laurendeau, *La crise de la conscription* (Montéal: Les Editions du Jour, 1962).
2. Ibid. 71
3. Ibid. 119
4. Ibid. 156, 157
5. Op. cit. 23
6. *Cité Libre* (Montréal: Le Syndicat coopératif d'édition *Cité libre*, avril 1962).
7. Ibid. 10
8. Jean-Charles Harvey, *Pourquoi je suis anti-séparatiste* Montréal: Les Editions de l'Homme, 1962).
9. Ibid. 15
10. Solange et Michel Chalvin, *Comment on abrutit nos enfants* (Montréal: Les Editions du Jour, 1962).
11. Ibid. 9
12. *Réal Caouette vous parle* (Montréal: Editions du Carroussel, 1962)
13. Ibid. 6
14. Ibid. 8
15. Ibid. 6
16. Ibid. 7
17. Ibid. 15

18. Paul Sauriol, *La nationalisation de l'électricité,* (Montréal: Les Editions de l'Homme, 1962), published in translation as *The Nationalization of Electric Power,* by Harvest House, in 1962.
19. *Pourquoi je suis séparatiste,* 9, 11, 72
20. The Nationalization of Electric Power, 14

CHAPTER SIX

1. *Report of the Royal Commission of Inquiry on Education* (Government of the Province of Quebec, 1963), p. 66
2. Ibid. 81
3. Ibid. 46
4. Ibid. 47-56
5. Ibid. 31
6. Ibid. 31
7. Ibid. 38-40-41
8. Ibid. 34
9. Ibid. 42
10. Ibid. 42, 43, 44, 53.
11. Ibid. 88
12. Ibid. 120
13. Ibid. 119
14. *Relations,* November 1963, p. 314
15. *Cité Libre,* November 1963, pp. 6–7
16. Paul Gérin-Lajoie, *Pourquoi le bill* 60 (Editions du Jour, 1963), p. 43
17. Ibid. 21, 22
18. Jacques Hébert, *J'accuse les assassins de Coffin* (Editions du Jour, Montréal, 1963)
19. Ibid. 54
20. Ibid. 17

THE QUEBEC REVOLUTION

Hugh Bingham Myers

Hugh Myers is a "typical English Canadian", as English as Cheshire cheese . . . . His father came from London and his mother from Derby. He grew up on an Alberta farm and graduated from a western university. In 1958, before the "revolution" he came freely to the famous Laval University summer school to study the French language.

In Quebec, he met and married a charming French Canadian girl. Hugh remained in Quebec City to teach English in the oldest boys school in Canada and to contribute two hostages — a son and a daughter — to the future of Canada. With these children, two more "typical" Canadians are amongst us.

It was a fair wind, in an hour of need, that brought us an author who contradicts in his person the stereotypes of bigots in all the communities of this land. It is insight of a high order that has led him to select so aptly the events that illustrate the power and acceleration which the "revolution" is gathering.

HARVEST HOUSE, MONTREAL